AF618146

Susan Hefuna

Anagrams

The British Museum, London
October 2022–2023

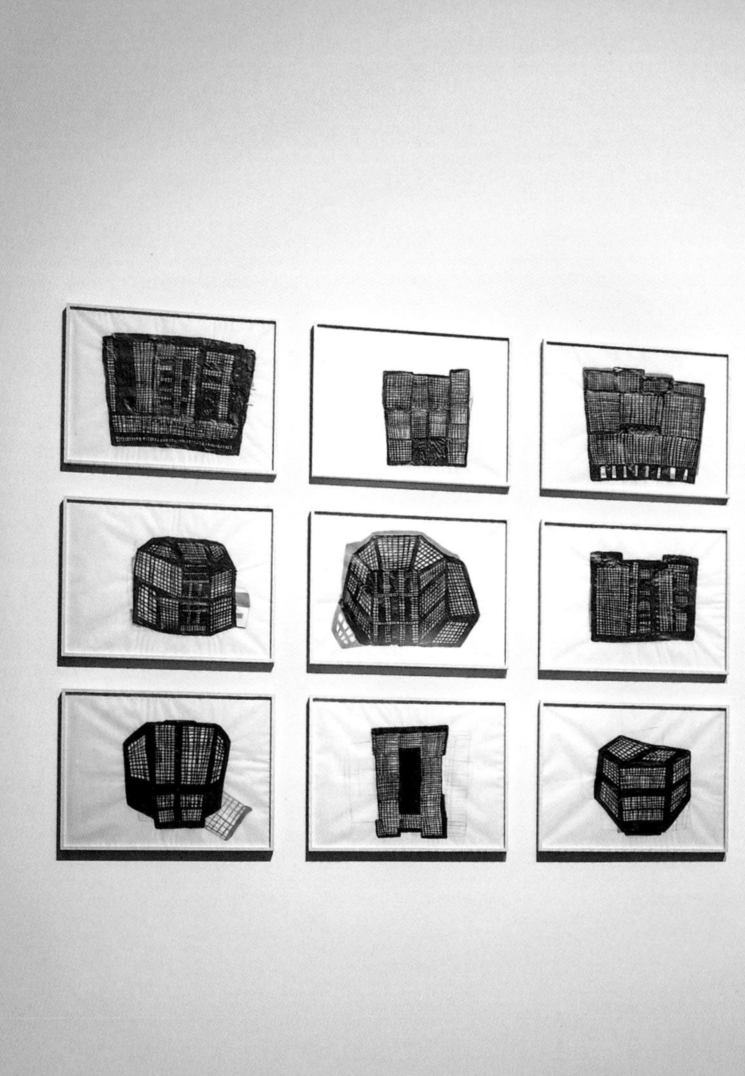

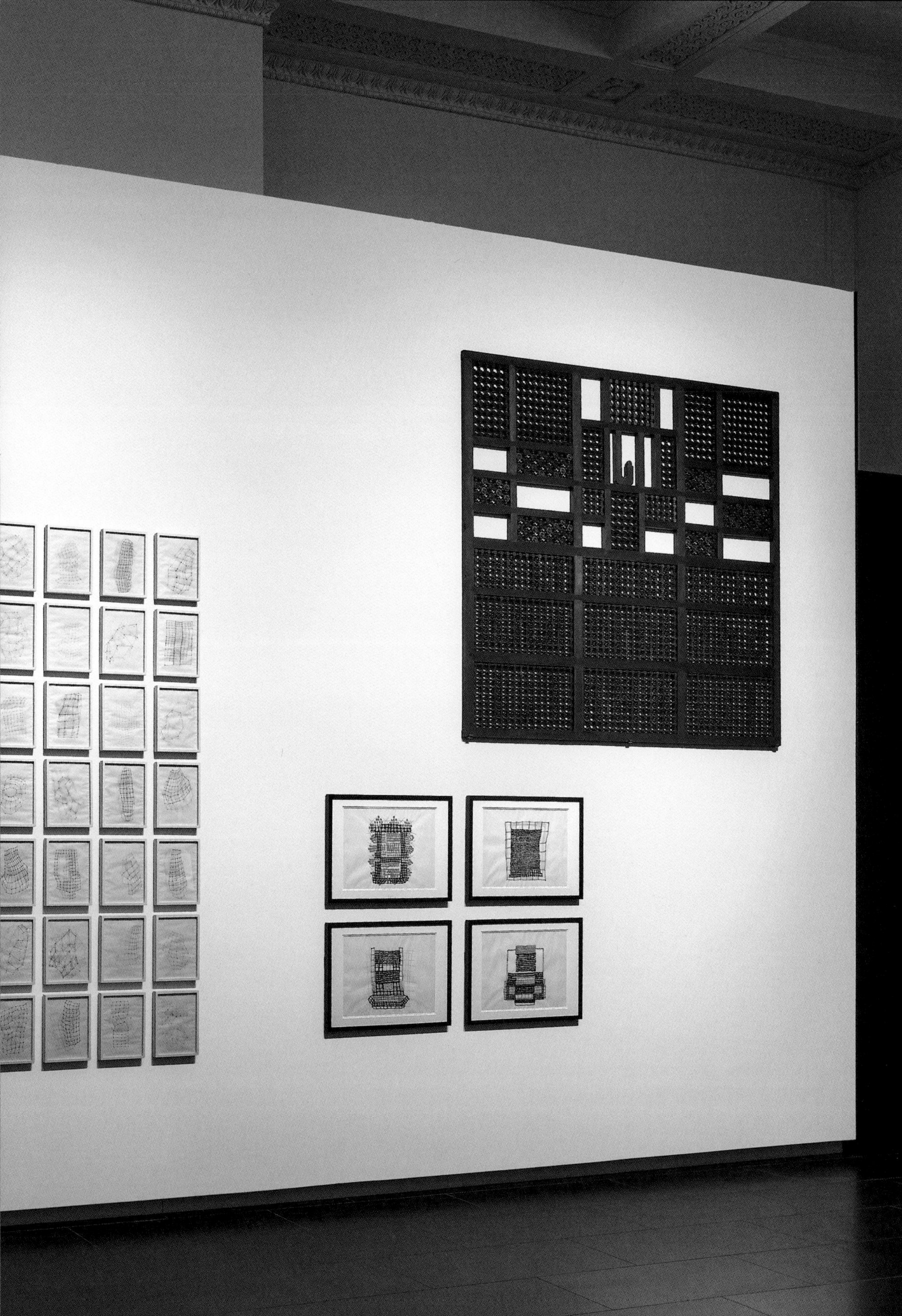

Susan Hefuna
Anagrams

KEHRER

Venetia Porter

Mashrabiyas and drawings by Susan Hefuna in the British Museum

An intricately carved wooden screen on a white wall. Within a tightly constructed grid, words appear, blur, and slide away as you get close. This is a *mashrabiya*, the screen that filtered the light in the traditional houses of Cairo, with different forms and names across the Arab world: *shanashil* in Iraq, *rowashin* in Jeddah. These screens helped circulate the air and enabled women to see out without being seen. The idea played upon the imagination of the Orientalists painters – Frederic Lewis and others – which Naguib Mahfouz turns on its head in *Sugar Street*, the final book of the Cairo Trilogy, by portraying the patriarch of the family, Al-Sayyid Ahmad, his declining years spent taking refuge behind the very mashrabiya that was, for his wife Amina, the 'outer limit of her world'.[1]

Brought up as a child in the Nile delta and returning to Egypt following her studies in Germany during the 1980s and 1990s, Hefuna encountered the masharabiya as though for the first time, becoming mesmerised by the beauty of these ancient traditional structures and excited by the abstraction within. She included some images of them in *A Cityscape Cairo,* 1999, a series of black-and-white photographs taken around the city made with a pinhole camera, and in her series *4 Women – 4 Views*, made in 2001, also using the pinhole technique, the mashrabiya is the background to her portraits.[2] It seems natural, therefore, that some years later, when invited by the Louvre in Paris in 2004 to contribute to an exhibition, she had resolved to interact directly with the mashrabiya and produce a work in wood.[3] She began to search for the artisans who still practiced the craft, and *Woman Cairo,* 2004, was the first in the series made of wood. Working with the Cairene craftspeople who have been in the business for several generations, further mashrabiyas began to take shape in which proverbs and single words were embedded into the screens. The three British Museum screens exemplify some of the different styles that were to become characteristic of her work: In *Knowledge is Sweeter than Honey (al-ma'rifa ahla min al-'asal)*, the proverb laid out in three lines is in the elegant angular style of the Arabic script that Hefuna favours for the texts (p. 65). *Ana*, meaning 'I', is a more complex composition. The word appears in Arabic and in both upper and lower case Latin (p. 71) across the different rows of varying size and shape. In *Hilm*, 'Dream', the screen itself has changed material, the turned wood structure now translated into bronze and the Arabic word whose sound alone evokes a dreamlike state, floats elegantly in the upper part of the screen. (p. 73). 'I often mix them up to create a new kind of language. Something may be written in Arabic and someone who could not read Arabic would only see a pattern without understanding the meaning, whereas the work would mean something totally different to an Arabic speaker.' 'The words', as she has said, 'are meant as an entrance for the observer and the screens are a kind of meditation for thinking about words. In principle they are just abstract screens, and everyone can just project something through the words.'[4]

Ana also reappears in *Anagrams*, a series of drawings exhibited at the Venice Biennale of 2009 at the main exhibition *Fare Mondi* and of which the British Museum holds 28 in its collection (pp. 31–57). An obvious question therefore is how do the drawings – with the purity of their minimalist abstraction – connect to the mashrabiyas? 'The drawings', Hefuna emphasizes, 'are not preparatory drawings for photos. [...] the drawings are the view I would have if I were sitting in one of these rooms myself, because the nice thing about these rooms is that you're isolated and protected from the world around you [...]. You see life outside the room, hear the cars, feel the hectic pace of the city – but you yourself are in calm surroundings, so it's therefore very meditative.'[5] *Ana* can perhaps be seen as a projection of the artist herself, a brief insight into the dichotomies of a peripatetic life since childhood: Cairo, Berlin, New York, and everywhere in between.

Drawing has been at the heart of Hefuna's practice since the early 1990s,[6] and, quickly, the drawings began to take on an architectural form, highlighted by the recurring use of the title 'Building', title given to both of the British Museum groups, made ten years apart. While the 2004 group (pp. 10–16) is closer to the mashrabiya, *Building*, 2014 (pp. 18–29), evokes Cairo, the density of the architecture and the city itself reduced to the essence. Layering is a key element of Hefuna's work: a first white paper layer is overlain by a second made of tracing paper; the black ink dots and netlike shapes appear boldly when at the top, as though in shadow when below. 'There is a dialogue between the drawings', she explains. 'When one layer of drawing is finished, it is complete and could actually stand alone but there is always an interaction with the next layer.'[7] She works intuitively, there are no preliminary drawings. Her mood is important at the outset, as she works on a drawing until it is complete. She describes it as a process akin to calligraphy. 'I have to retreat into my shell to create these series. What happens is, every so often I take a break, and then an entire series is born. So if there is a phase with the right atmosphere and if I'm able to withdraw, then I need a few days before I can actually begin to draw.'[8] Each of the groups illustrated here takes on its own character. In the 28 drawings of *Anagram*, combining the words 'Ana' and 'Anagram', entirely drawn with pencil on the layers of tracing paper, the shapes guided by fixed points, a pale red occasionally emerges. There are letters and numbers, as though alluding to a mysterious magical formula. Hefuna calls these drawings 'a poem in variation', an apt description of all the art she makes.

1 Naguib Mahfouz, *Sugar Street: The Cairo Trilogy III* Translated by William Maynard Hutchings and Angele Botros Samaan (New York: Anchor Books 1957 (Kindle edition)), p. 212.
2 Susan Hefuna, *Xcultural Codes* (Kehrer 2004), pp. 66ff. See also Vassilis Oikonomopoulos 'Another geometry: Hefuna's exploration of the line' in *Susan Hefuna: Drawing Everything* (New York: The Drawing Center 2020), pp. 11–16.
3 Woman Cairo-2004 was shown in *Contrepoints,* Louvre, Paris, 2004–2005
4 Hans Ulrich Obrist, (ed.) *Susan Hefuna: Pars Pro Toto II* (Heidelberg: Kehrer 2009), p. 162
5 Hans Ulrich Obrist, (ed.) *Susan Hefuna: Pars Pro Toto* (Heidelberg: Kehrer 2008), p. 13
6 Brett Littman (ed.) *Drawing Everything* (New York: The Drawing Centre 2020)
7 Hans Ulrich Obrist, (ed.) *Susan Hefuna: Pars Pro Toto II* (Heidelberg: Kehrer 2009), p. 159
8 Hans Ulrich Obrist, (ed.) *Susan Hefuna: Pars Pro Toto* (Heidelberg: Kehrer 2008), p. 14

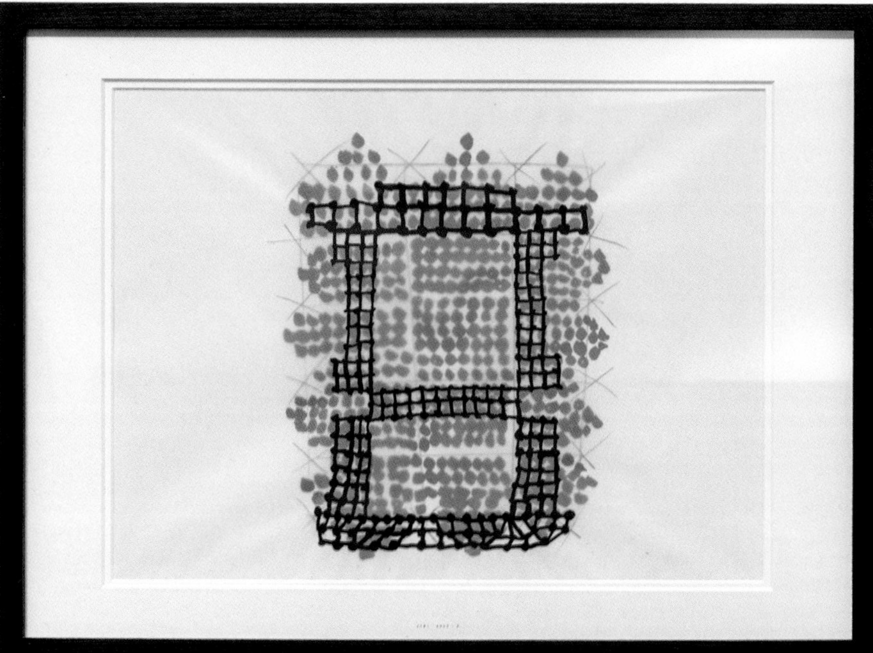

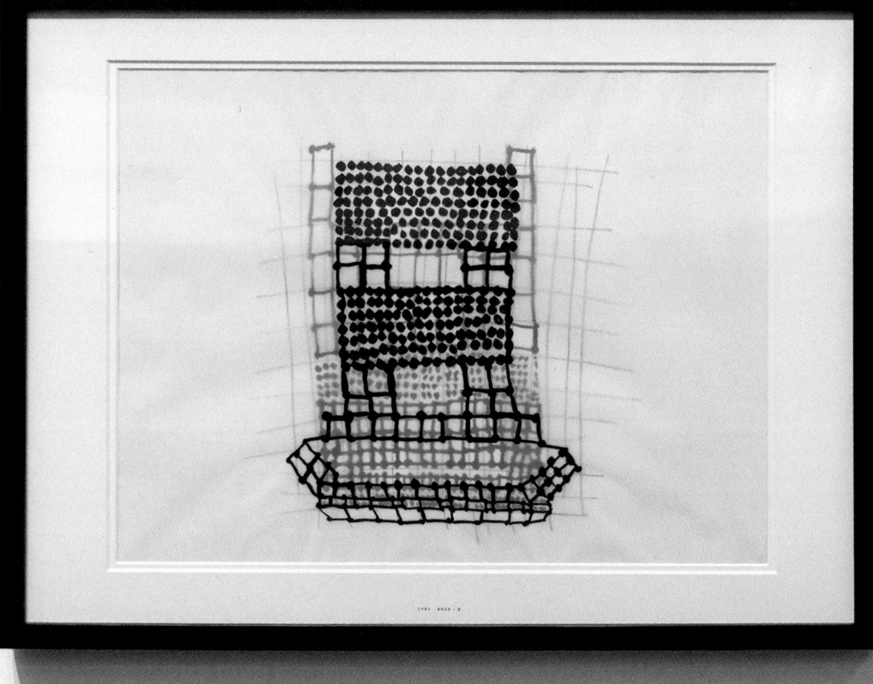

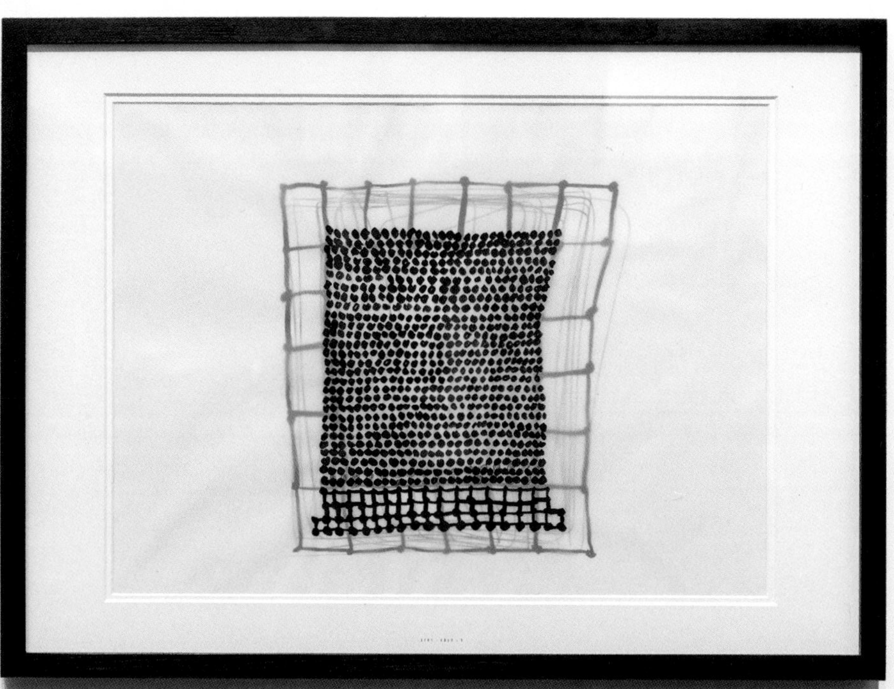

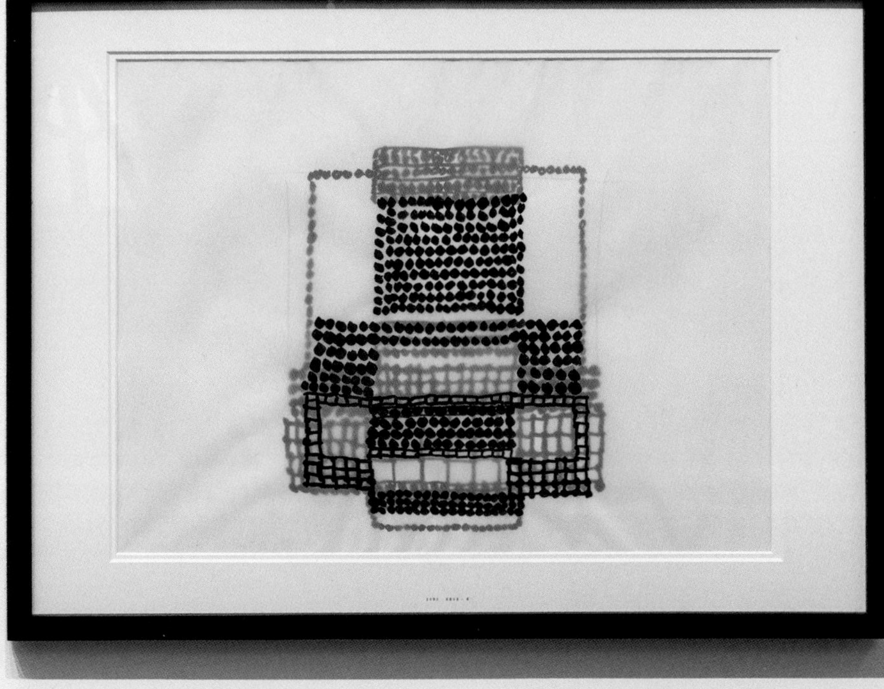

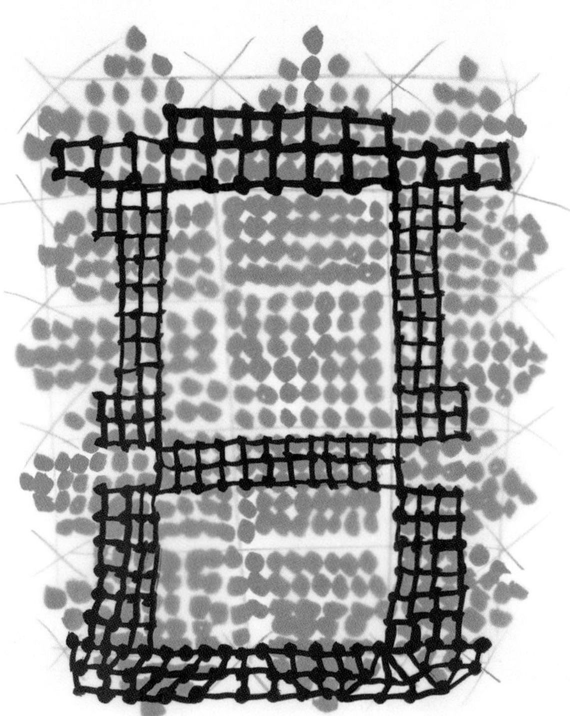

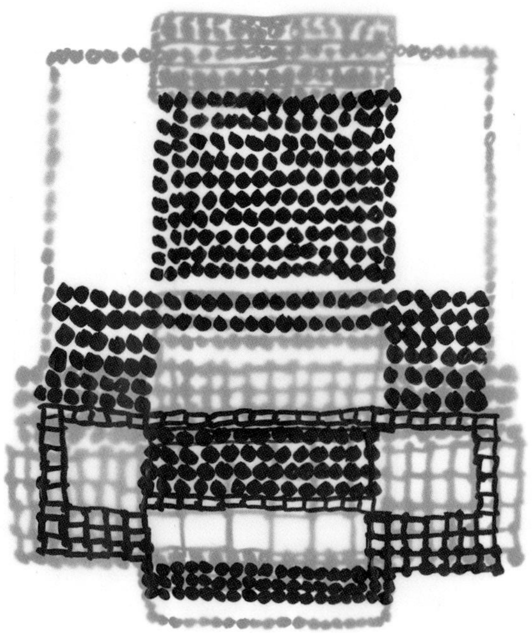

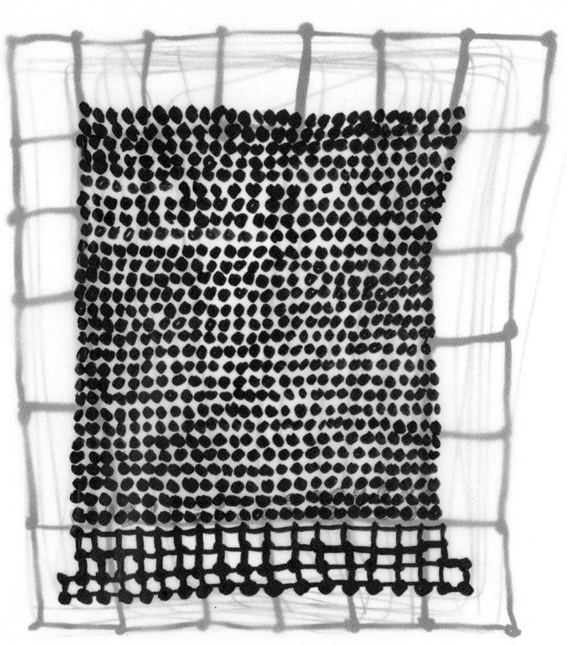

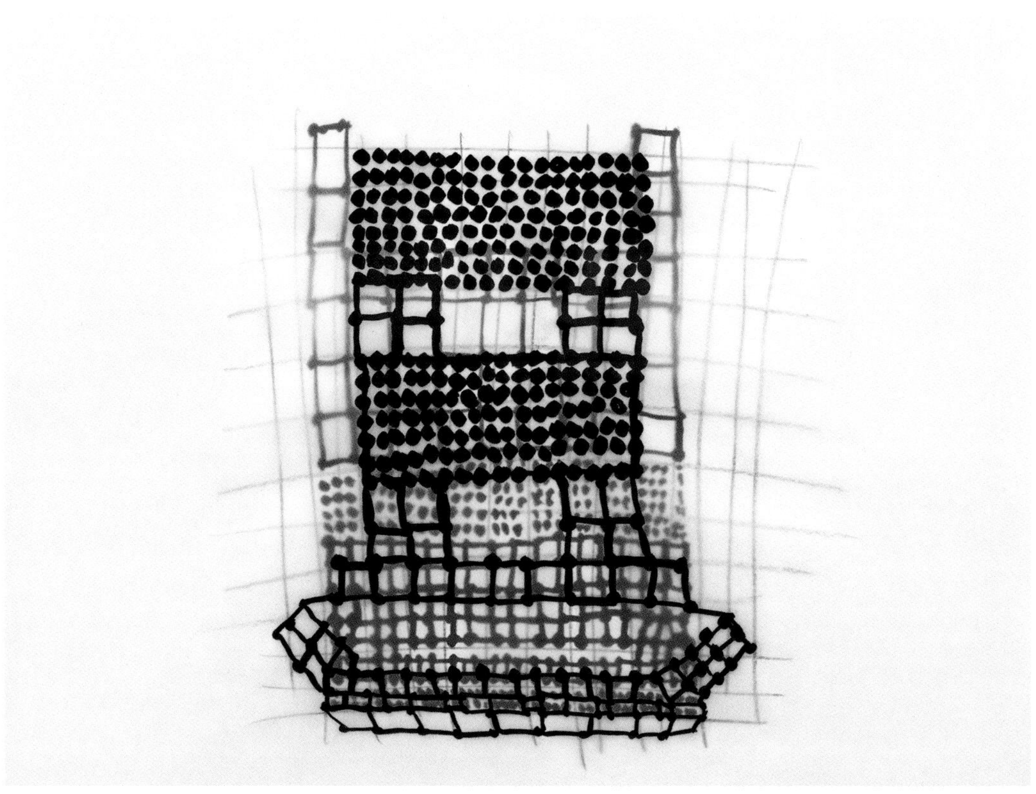

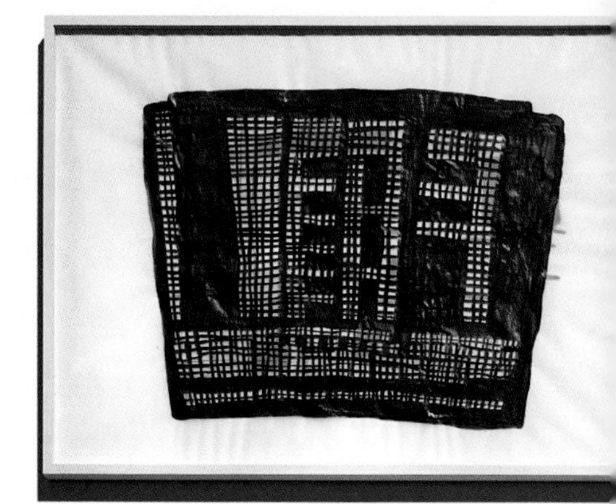

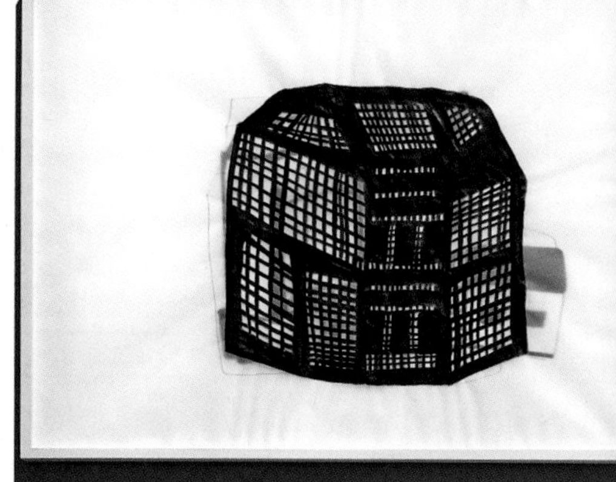

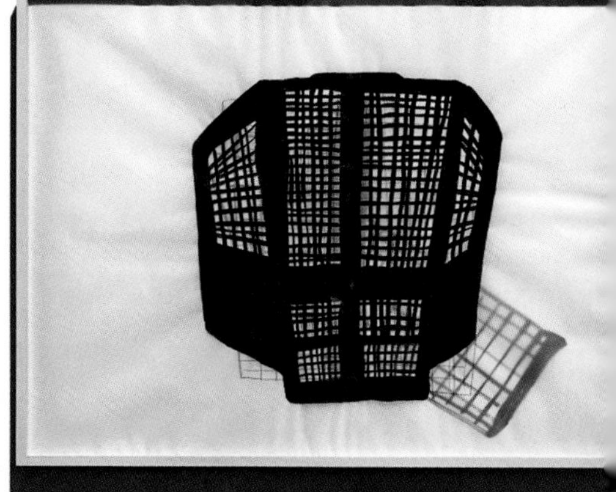

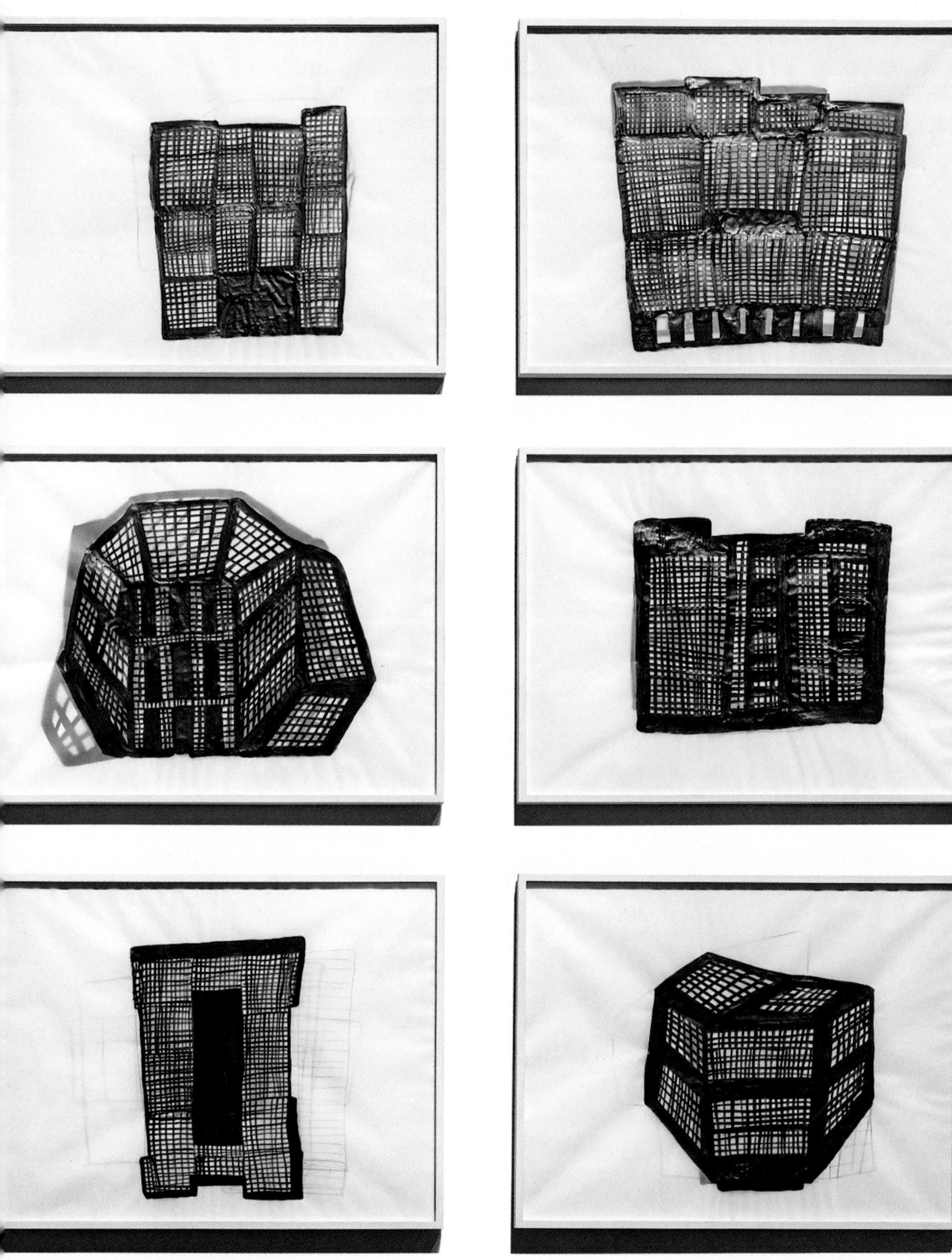

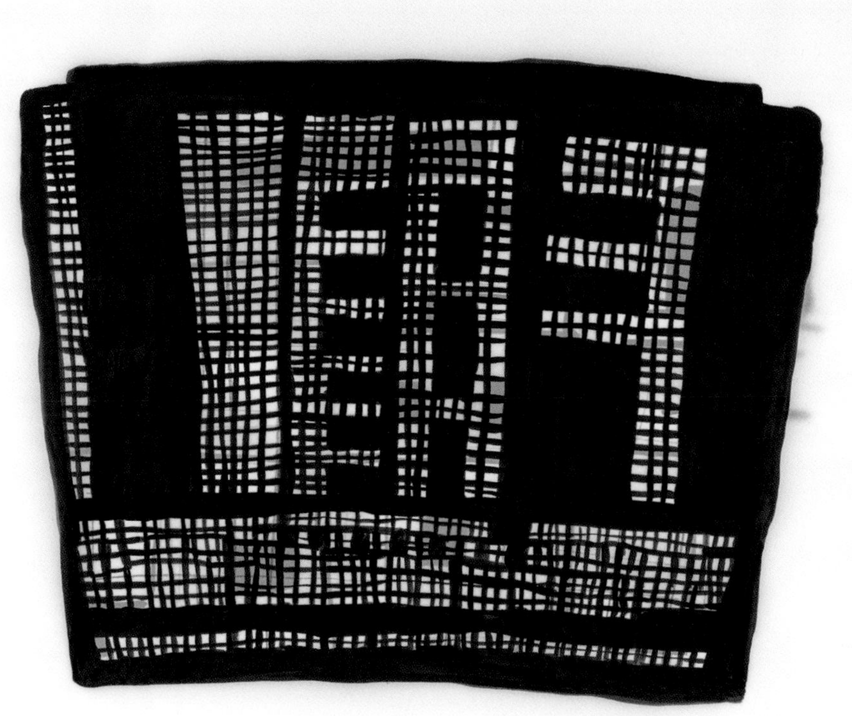

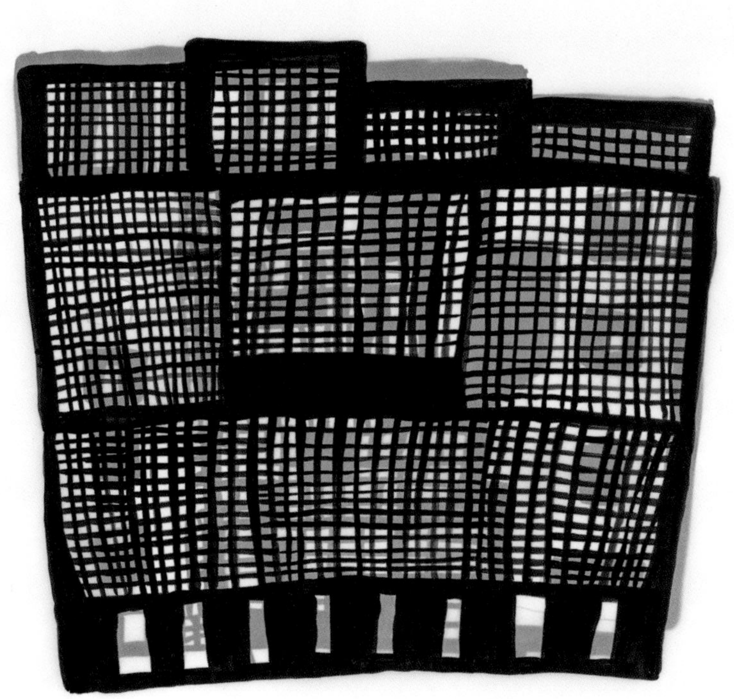

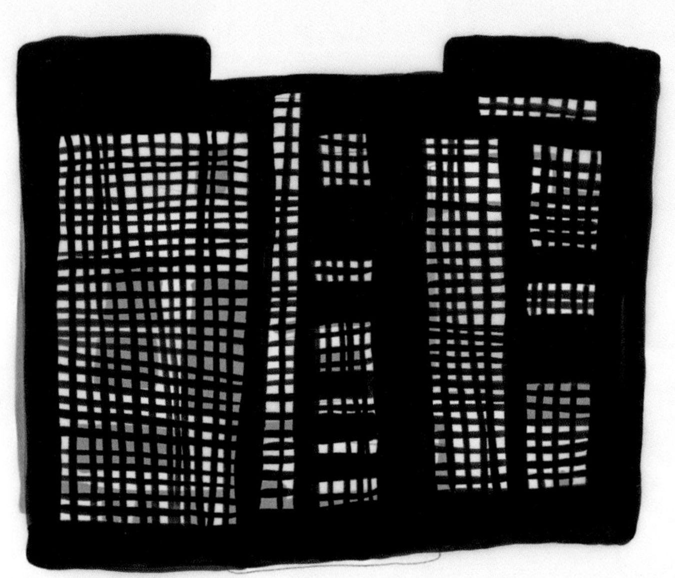

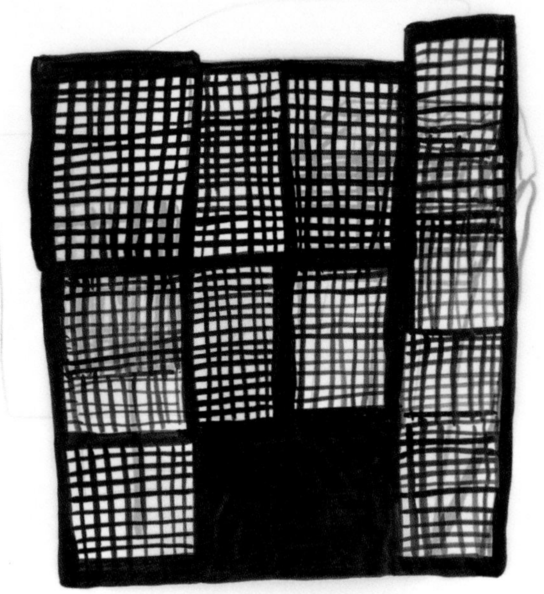

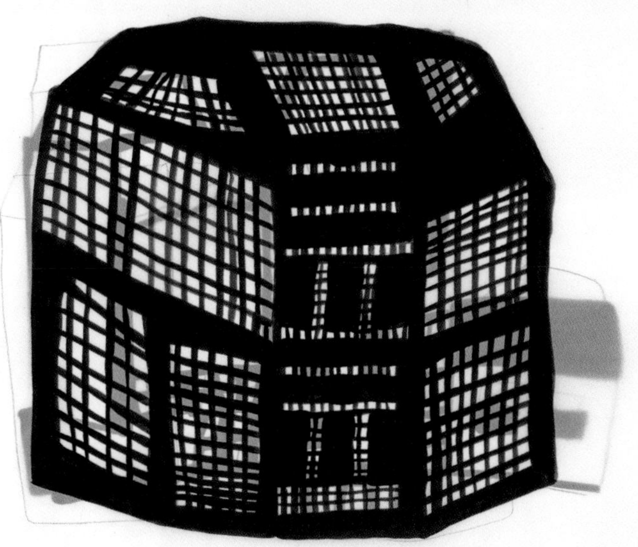

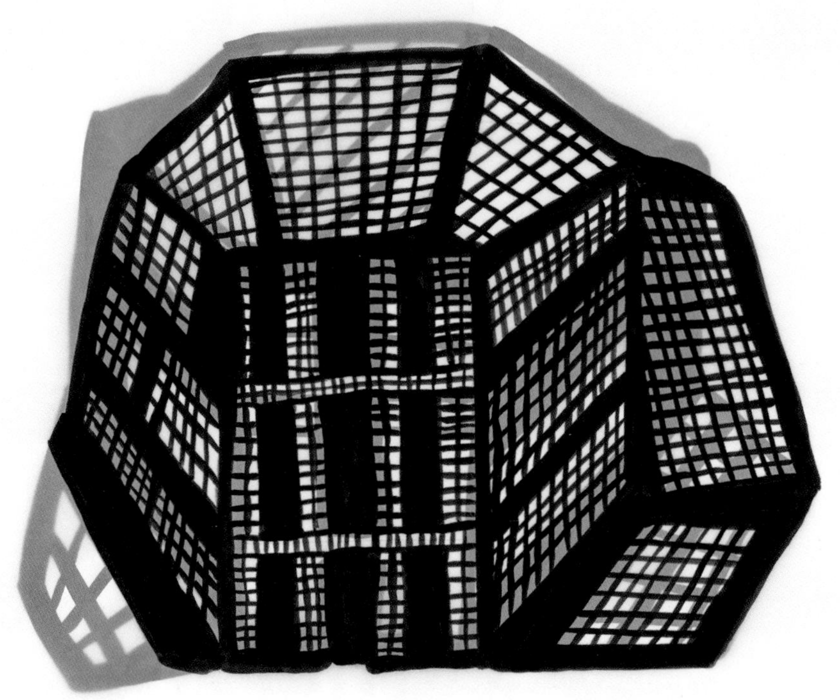

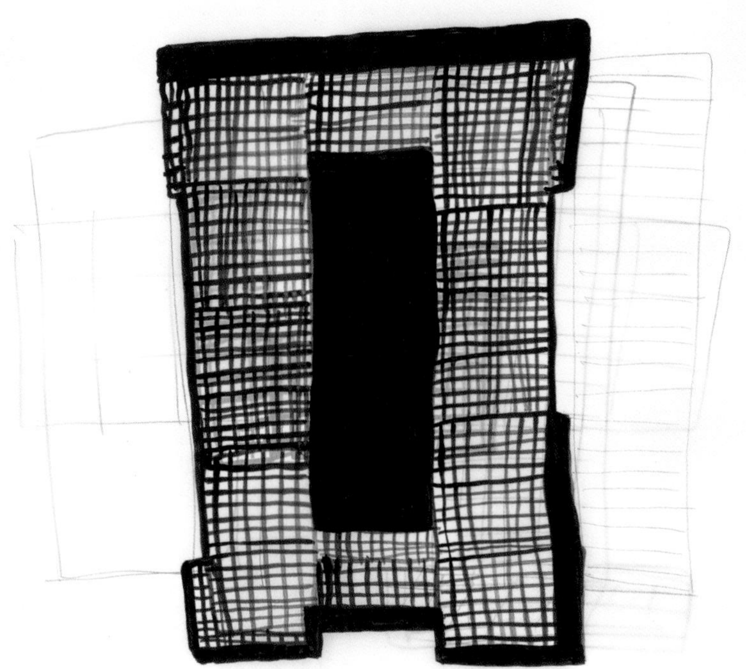

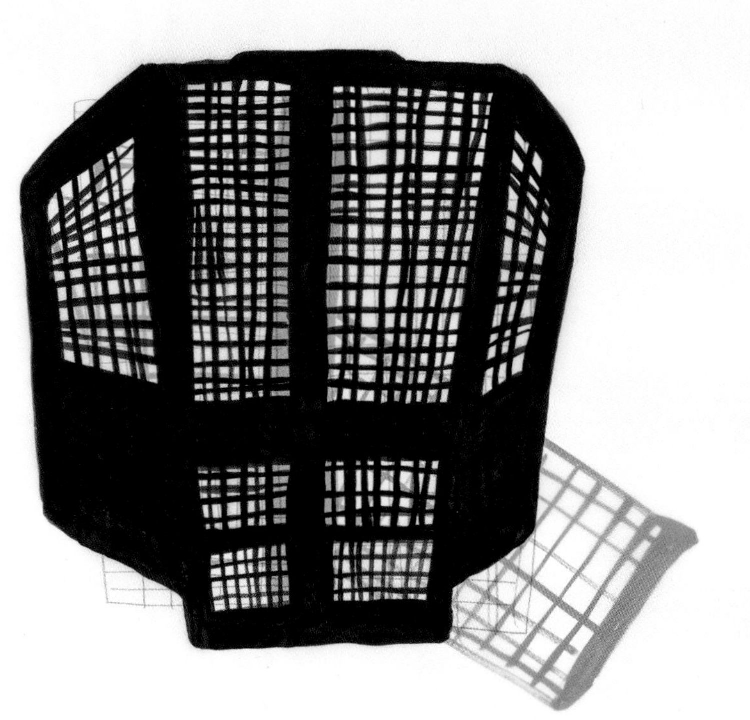

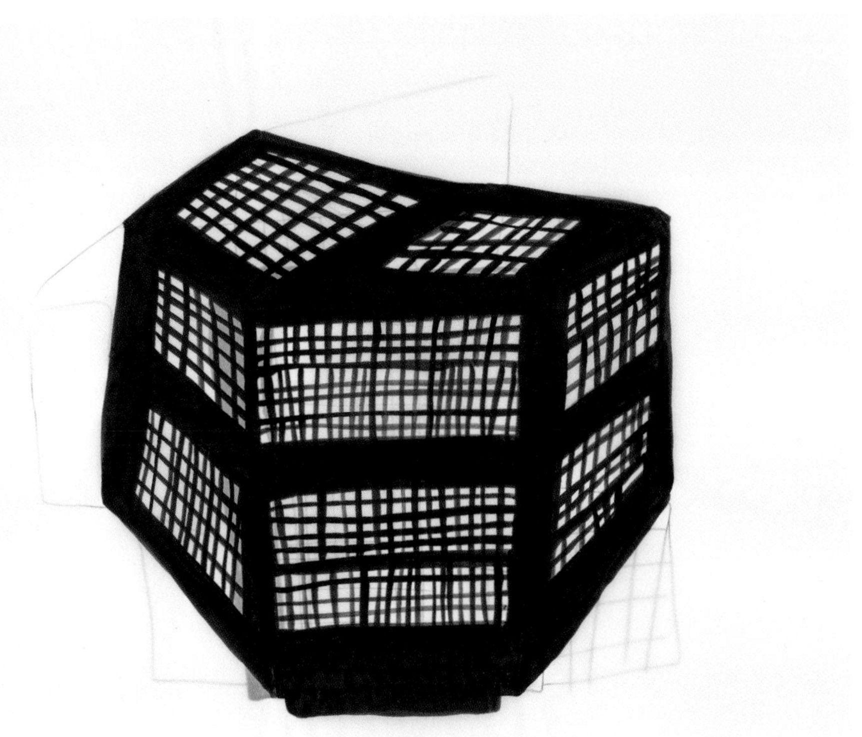

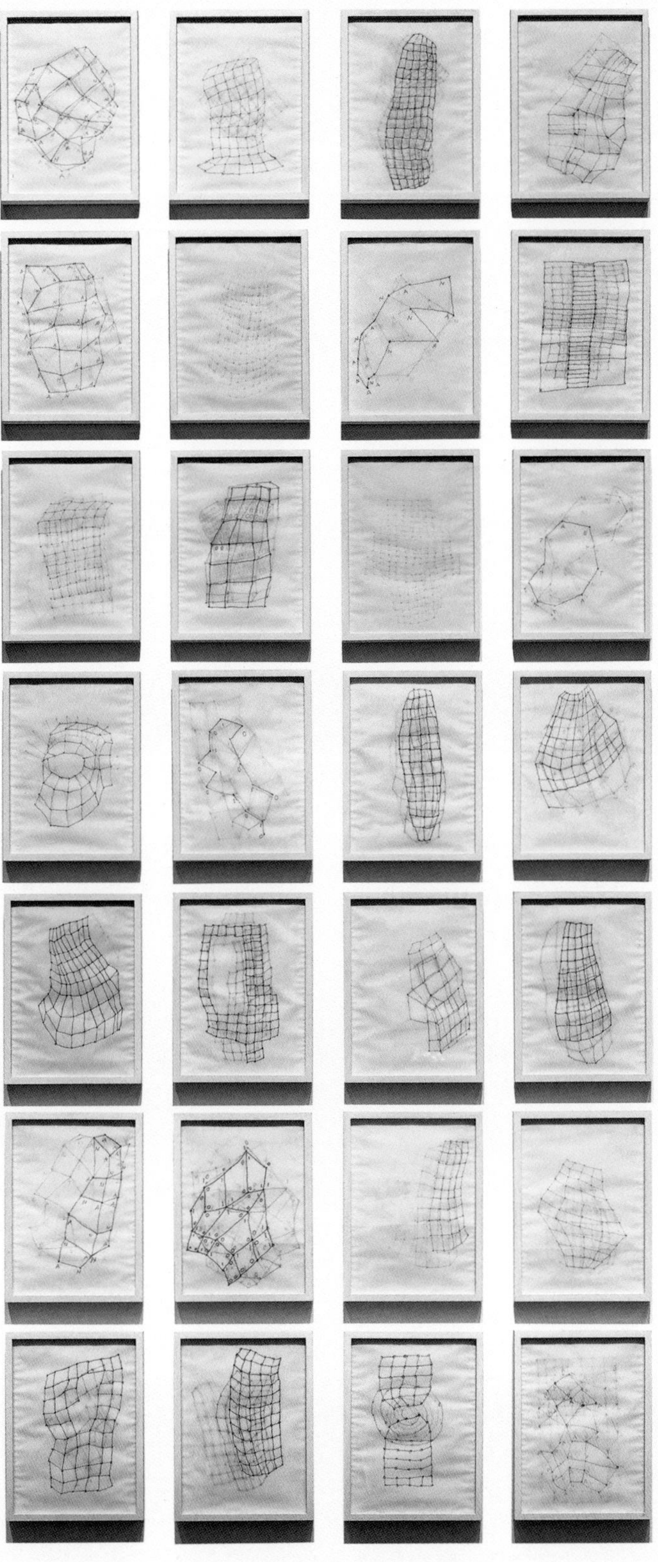

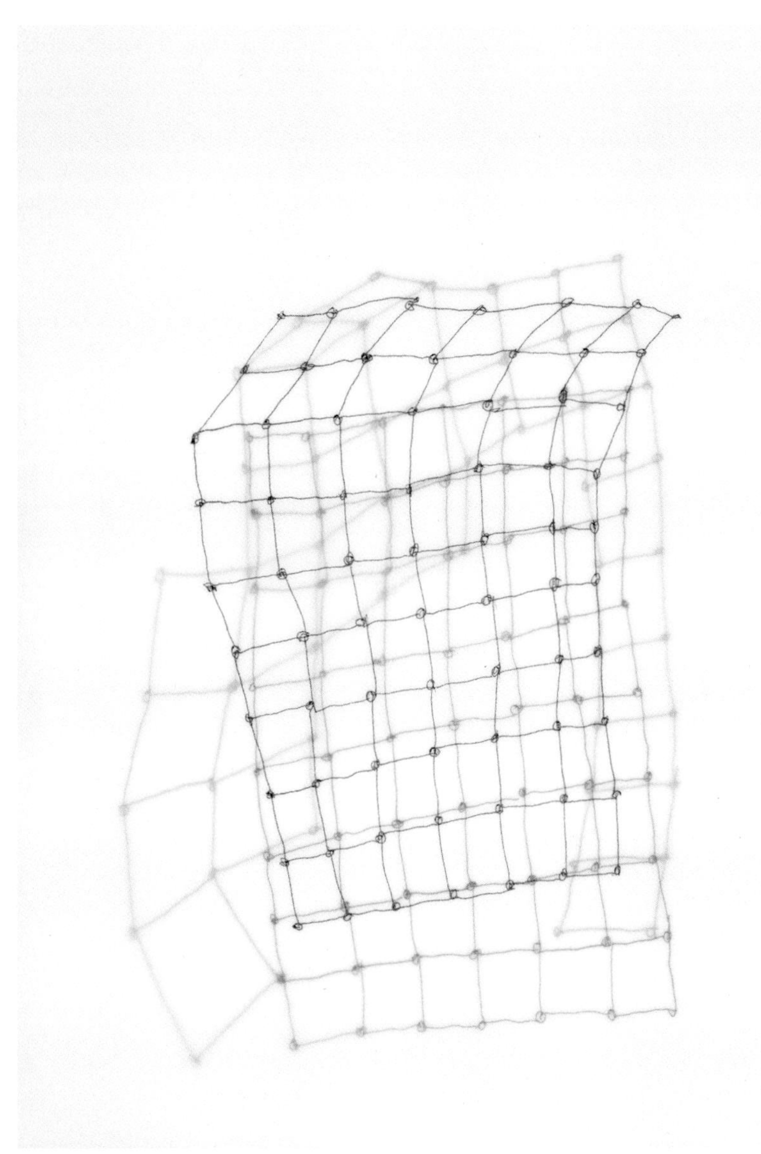

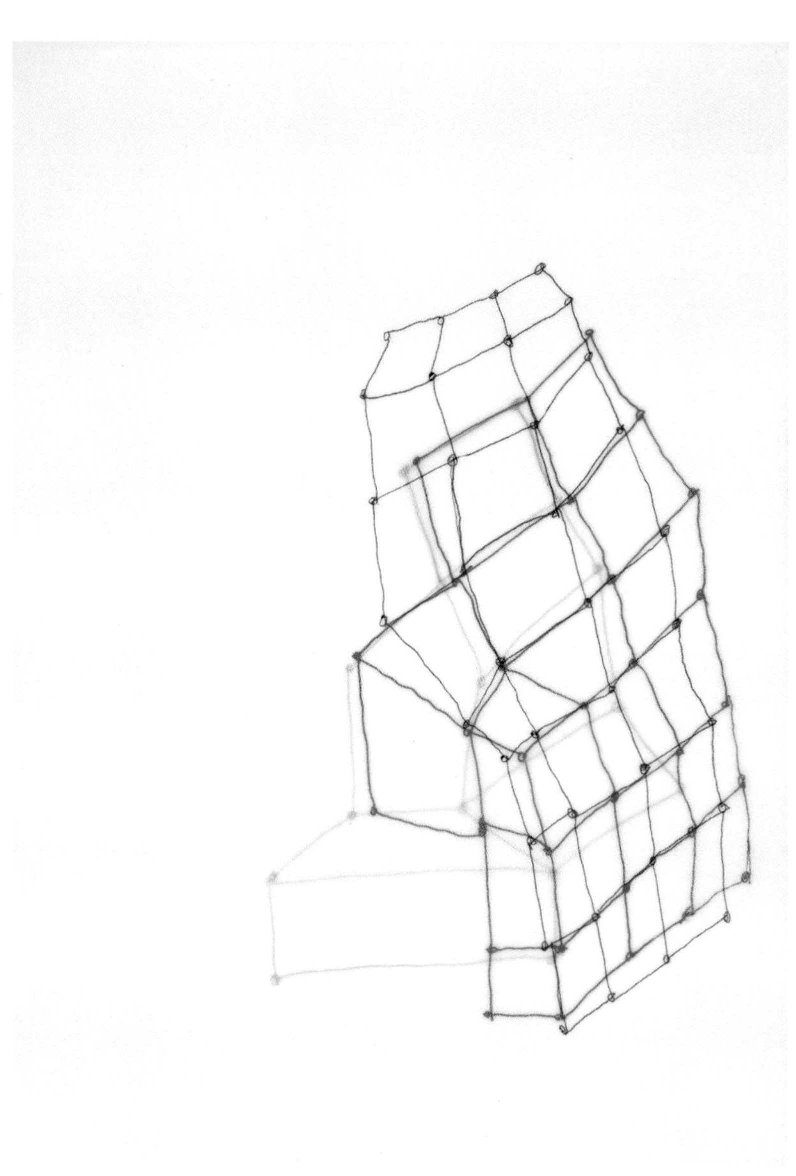

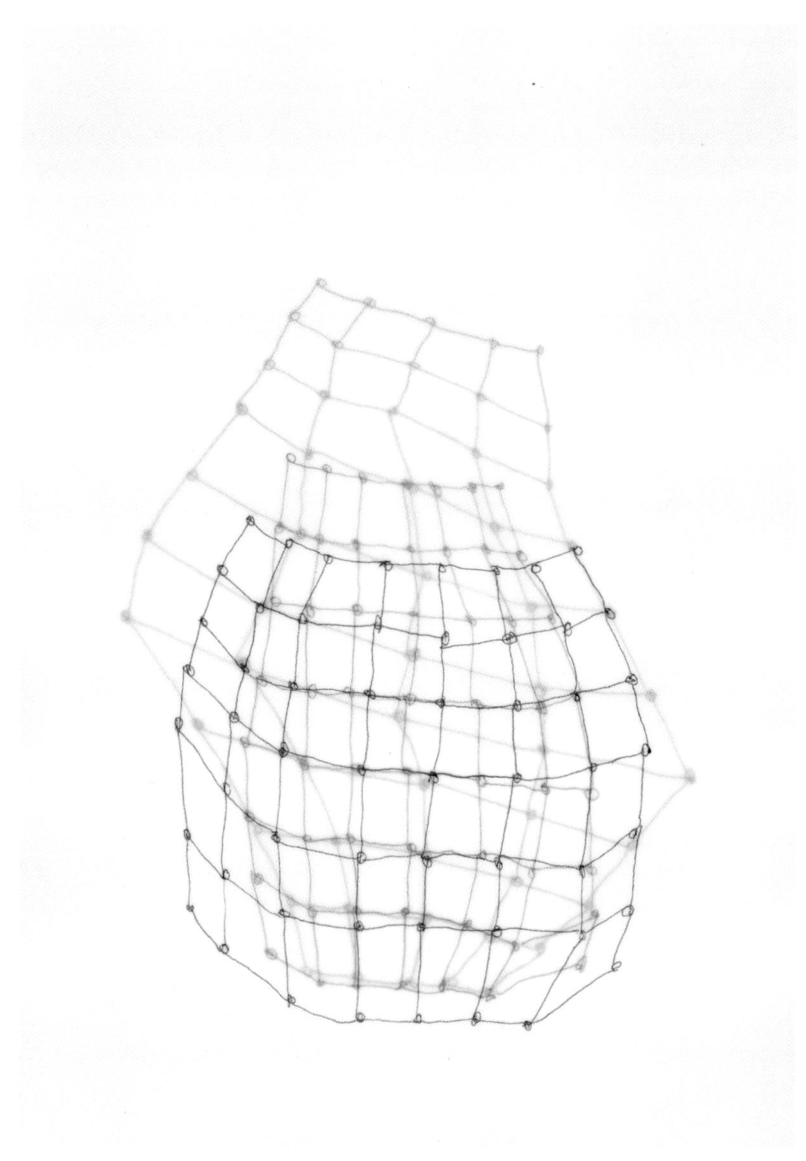

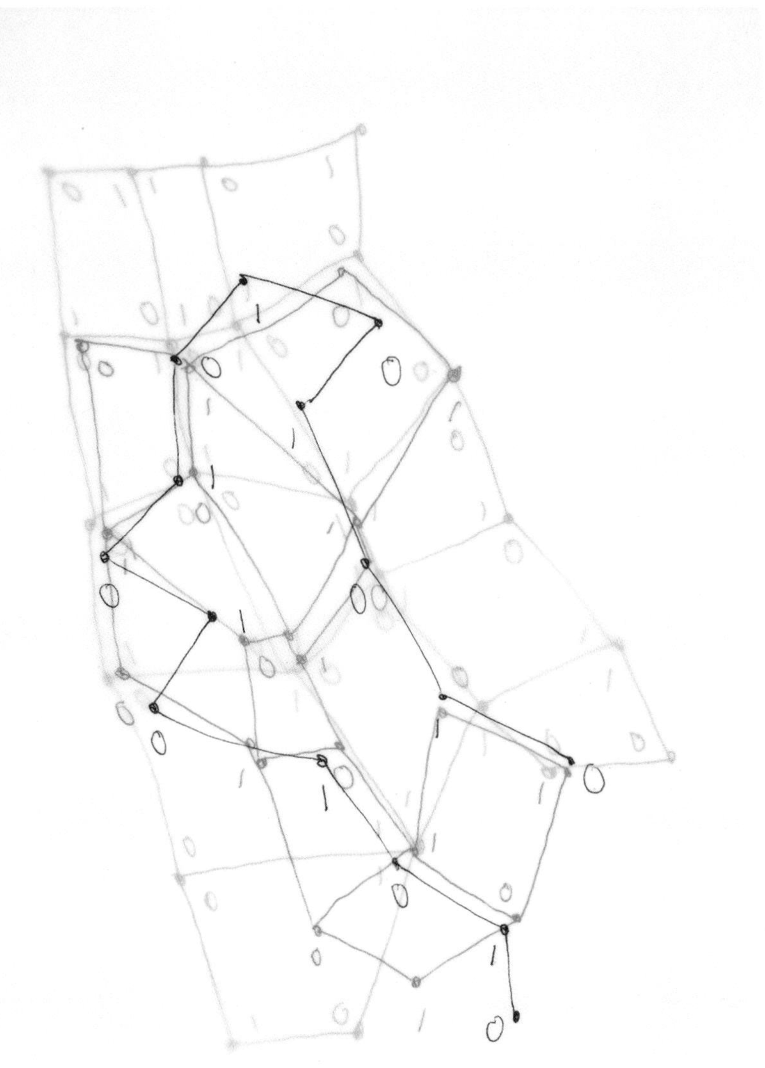

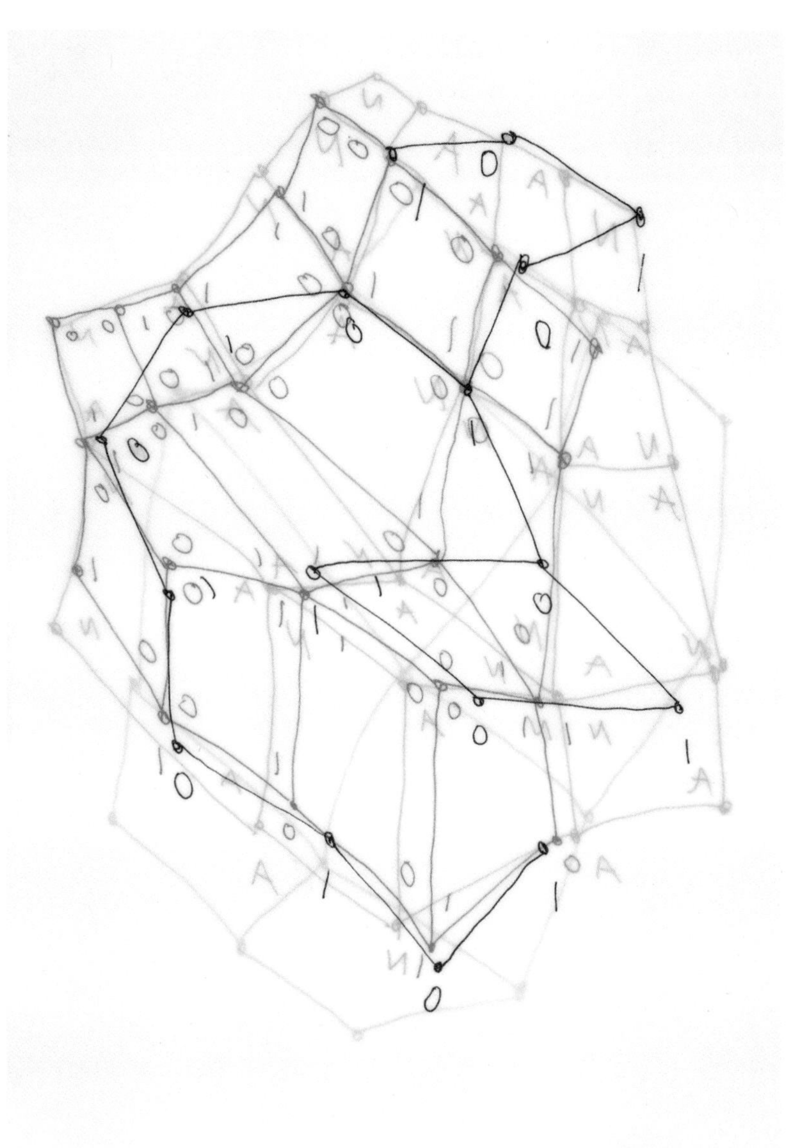

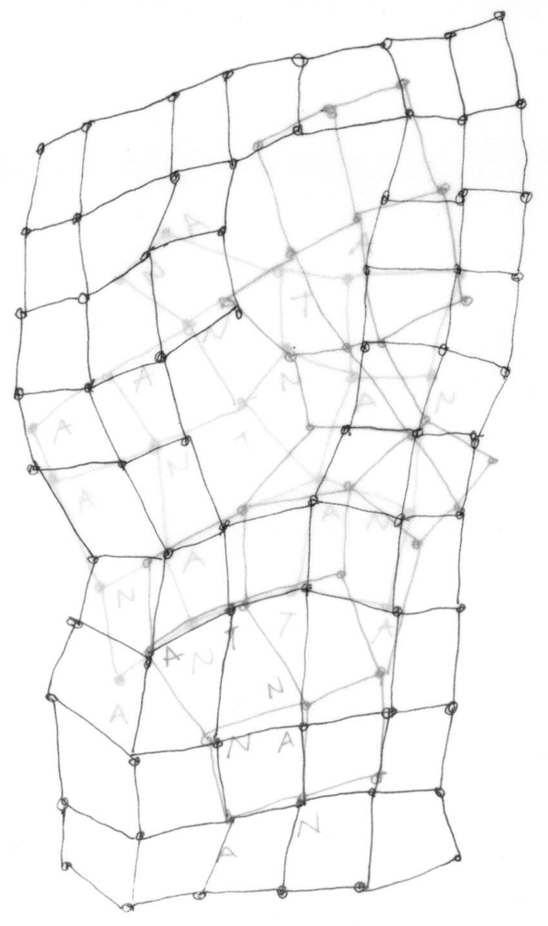

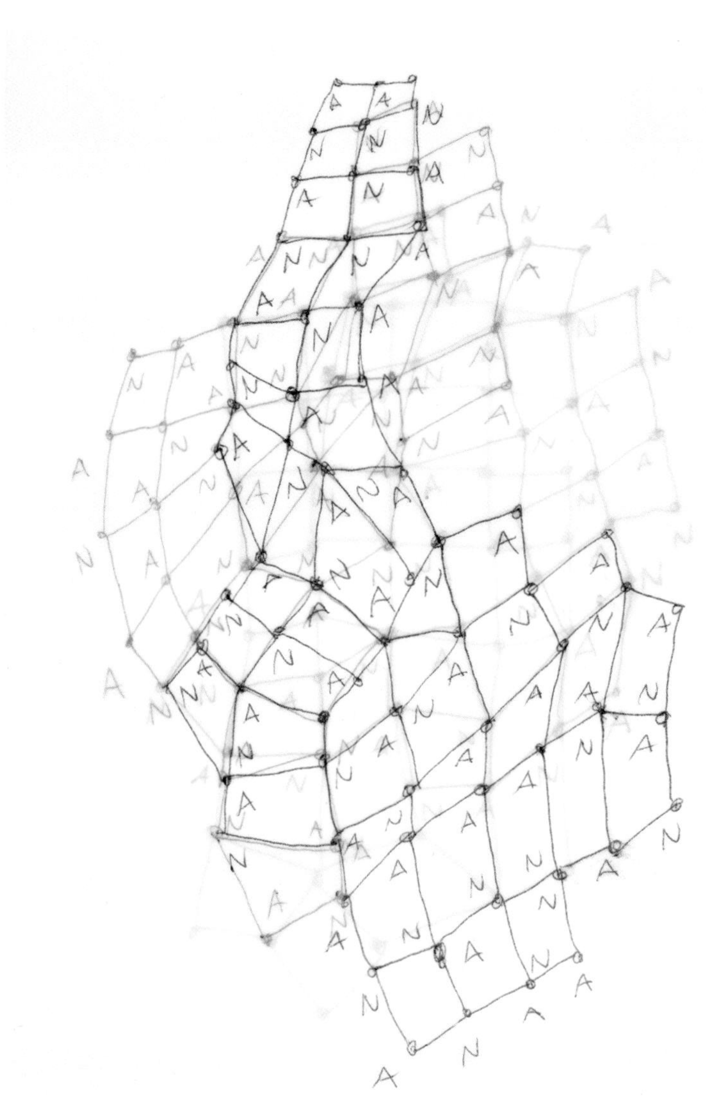

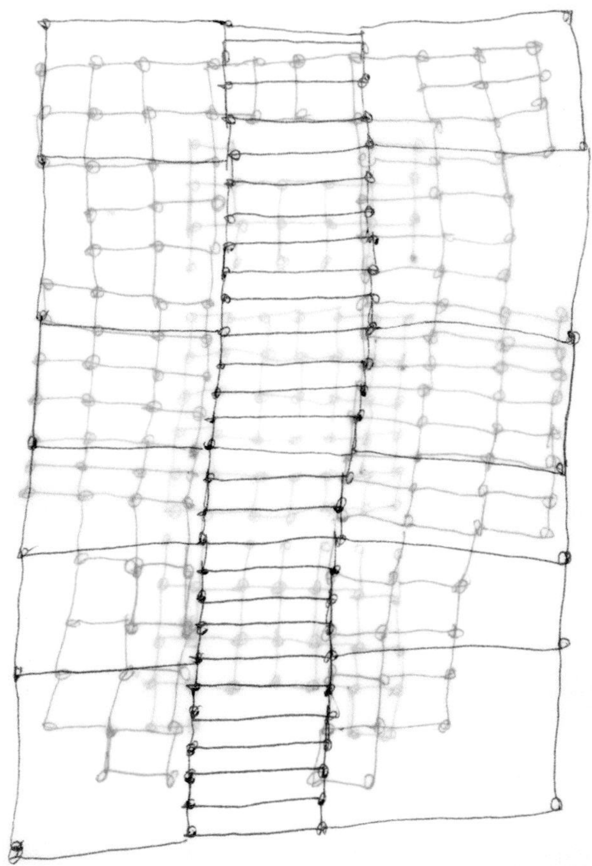

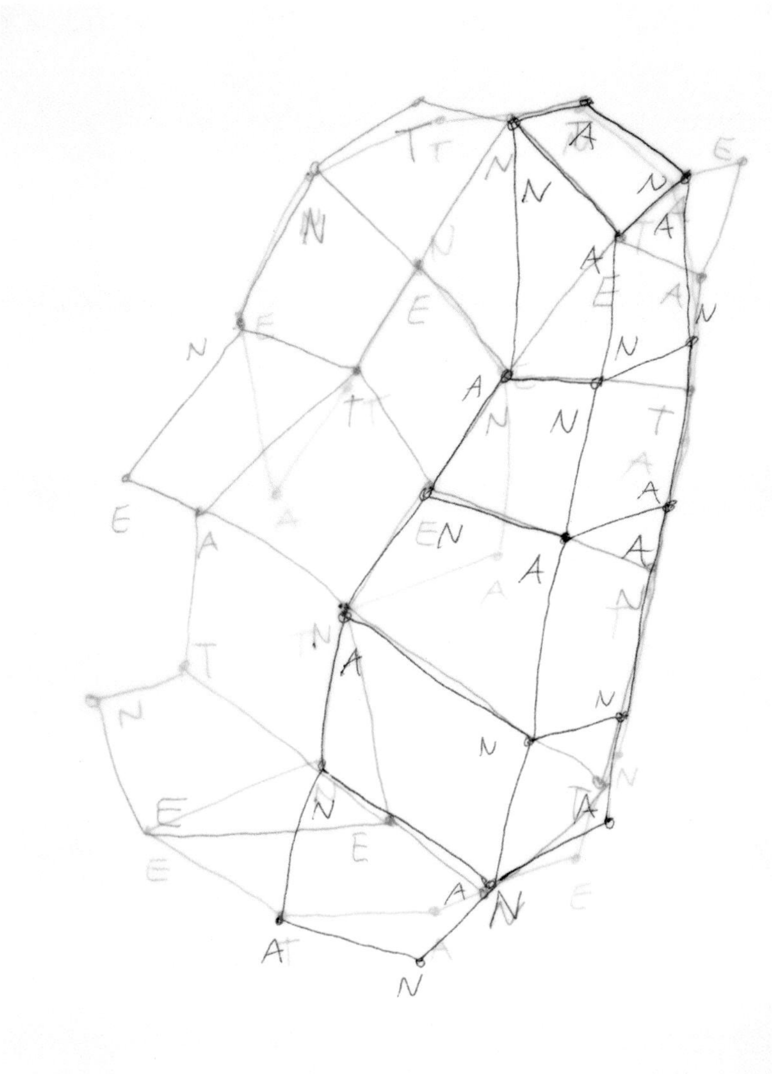

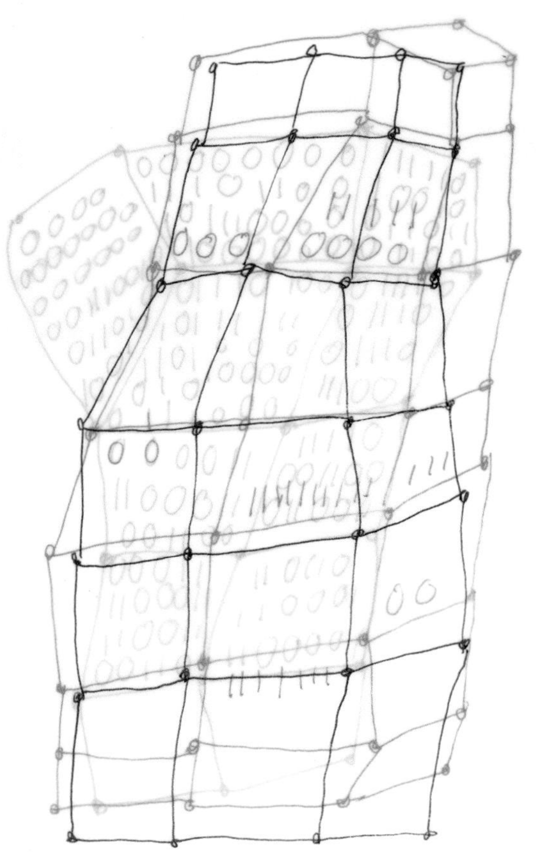

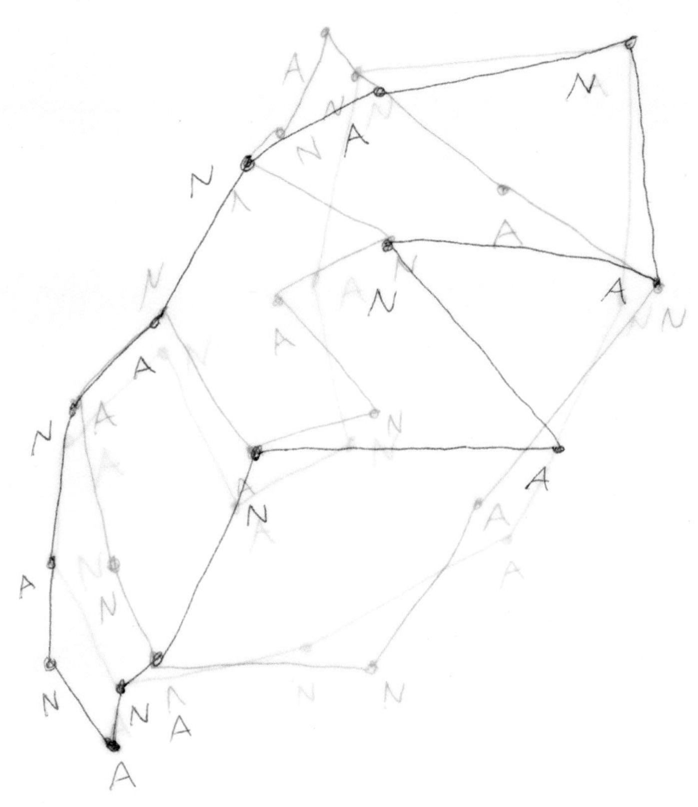

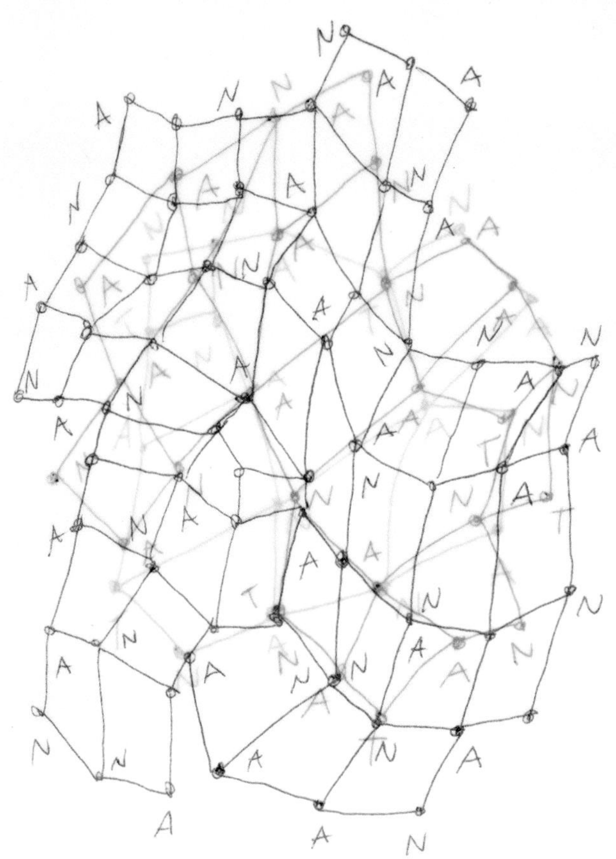

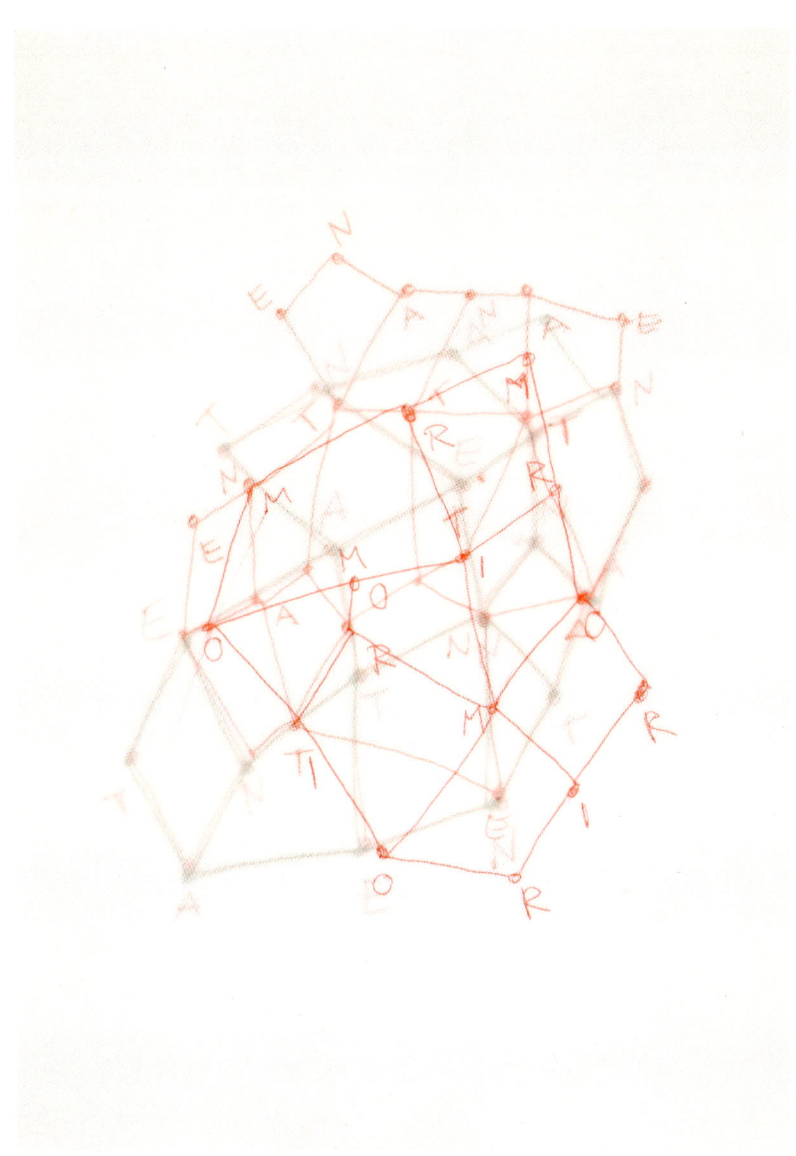

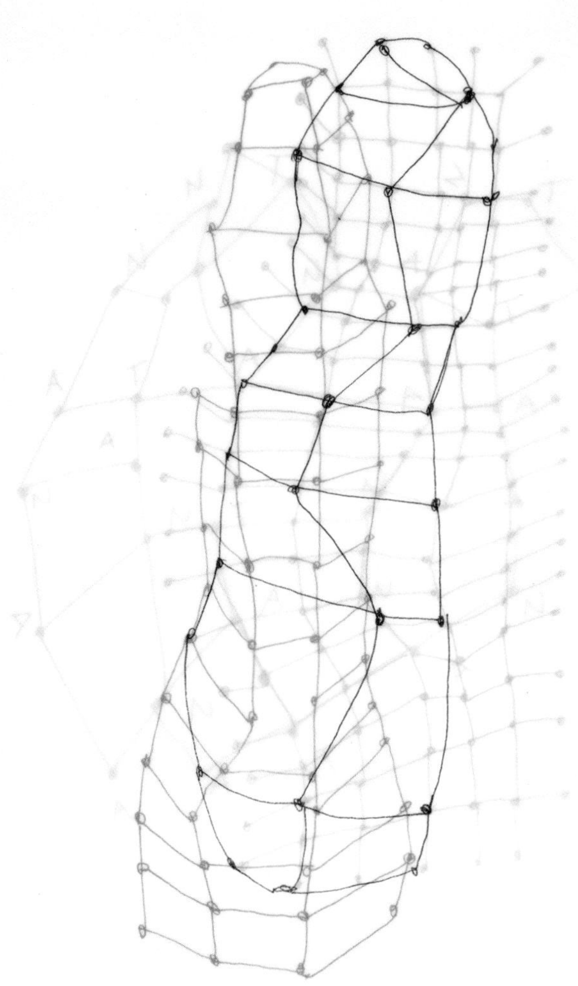

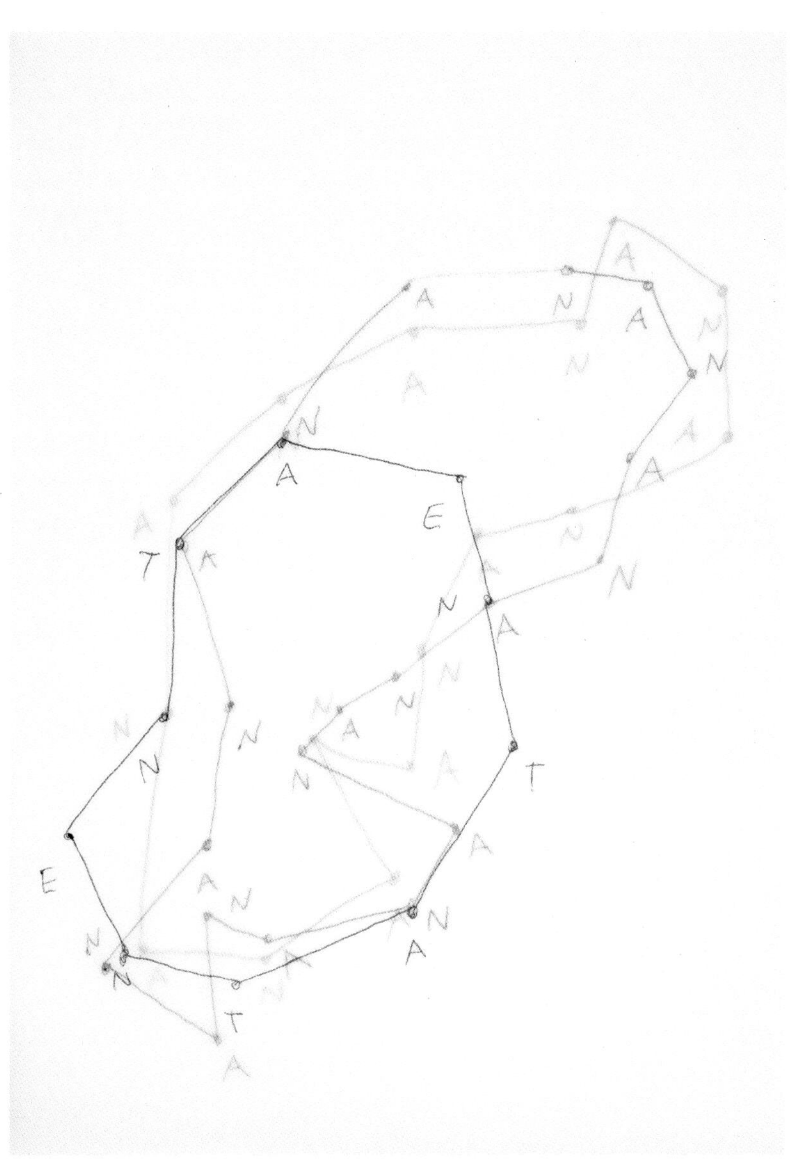

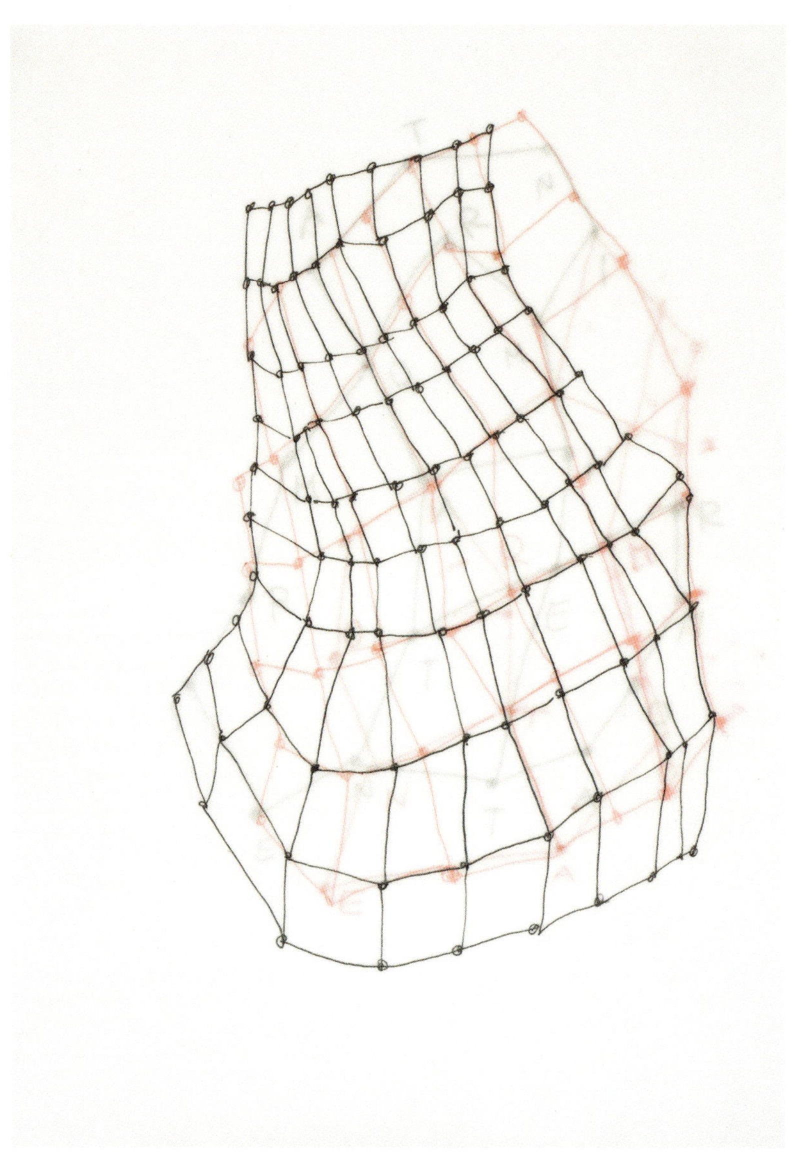

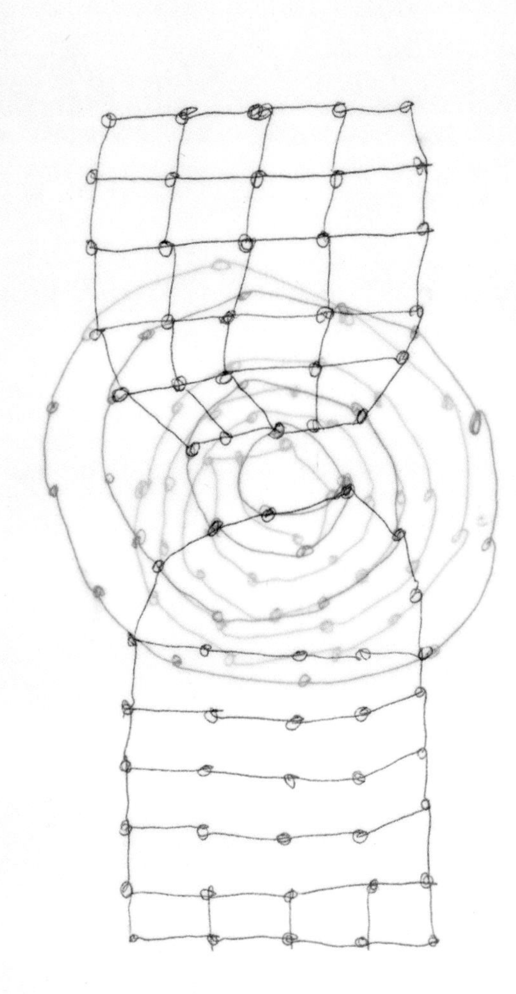

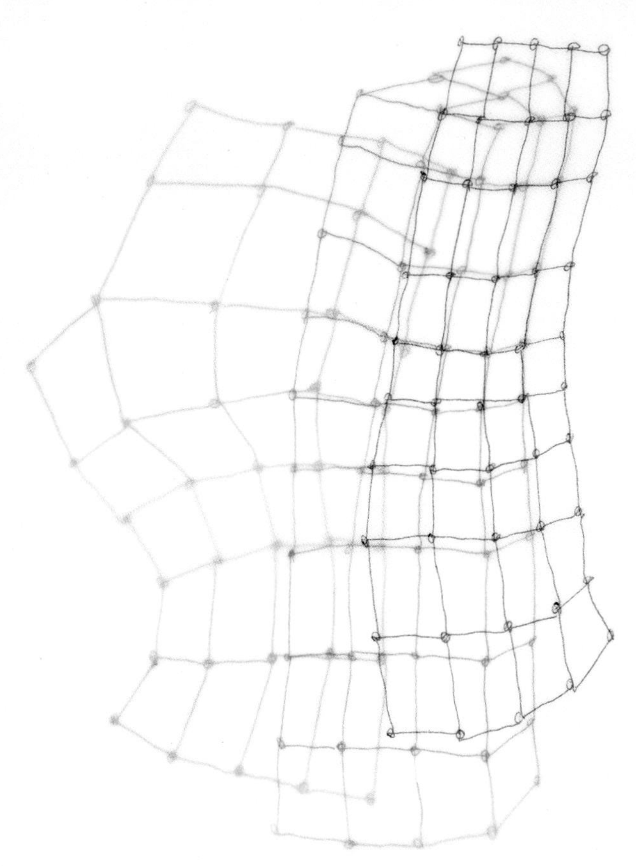

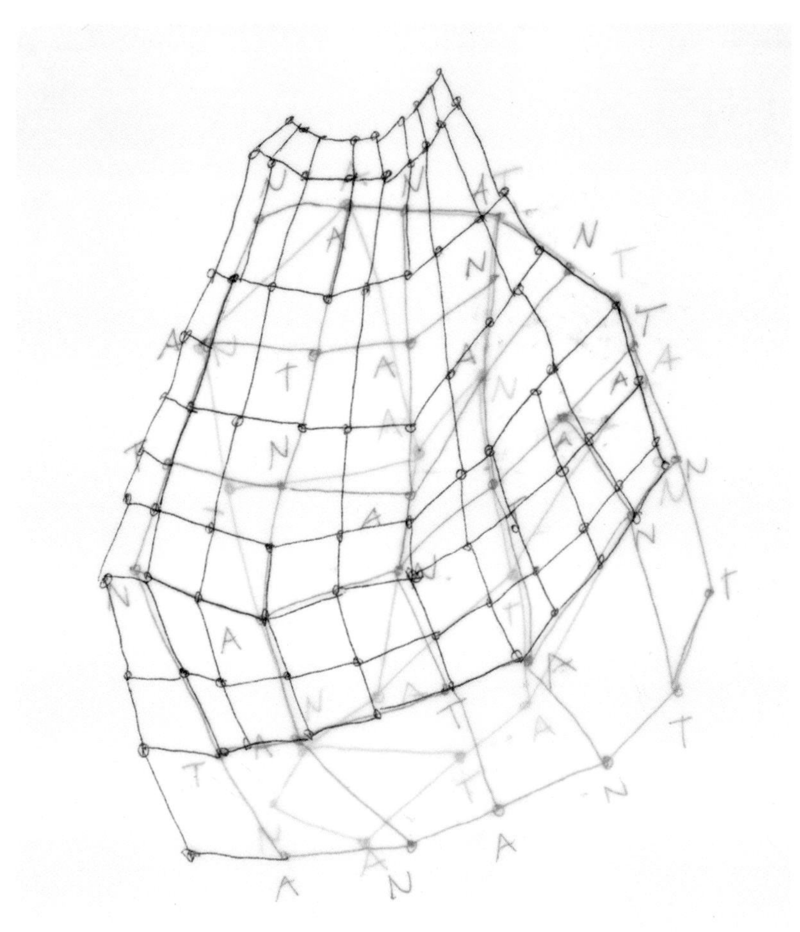

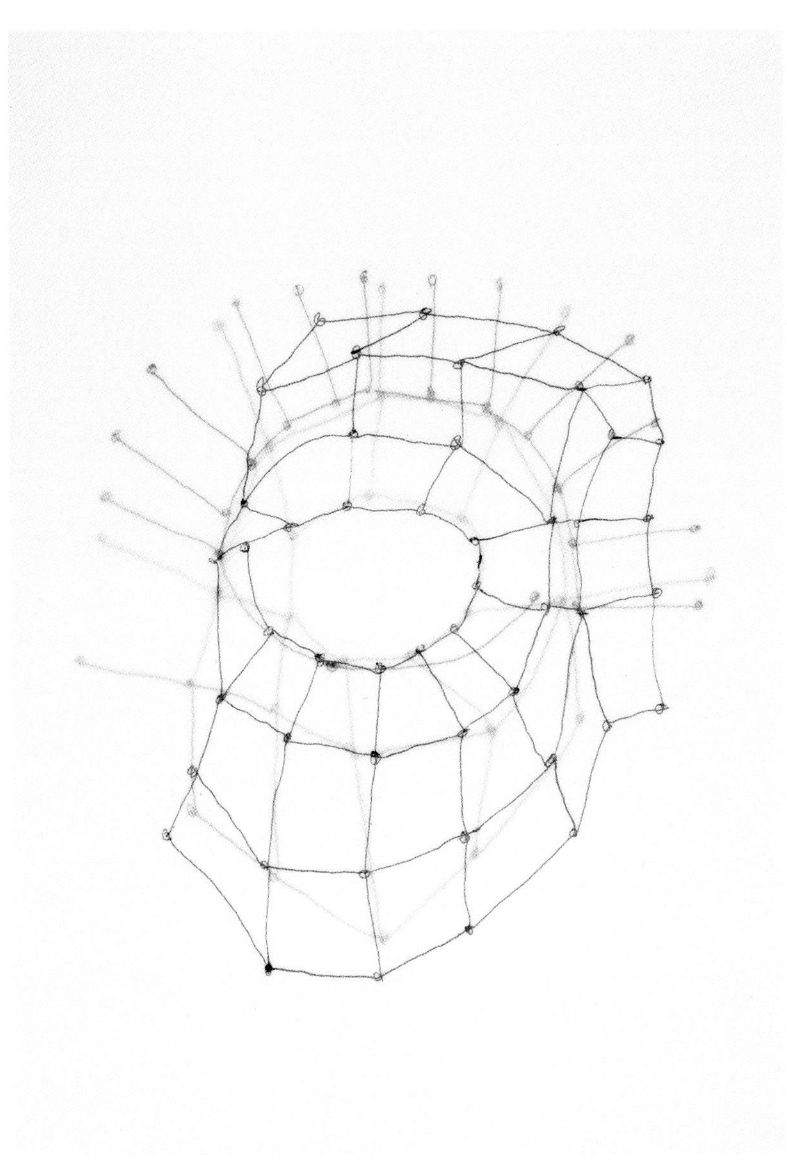

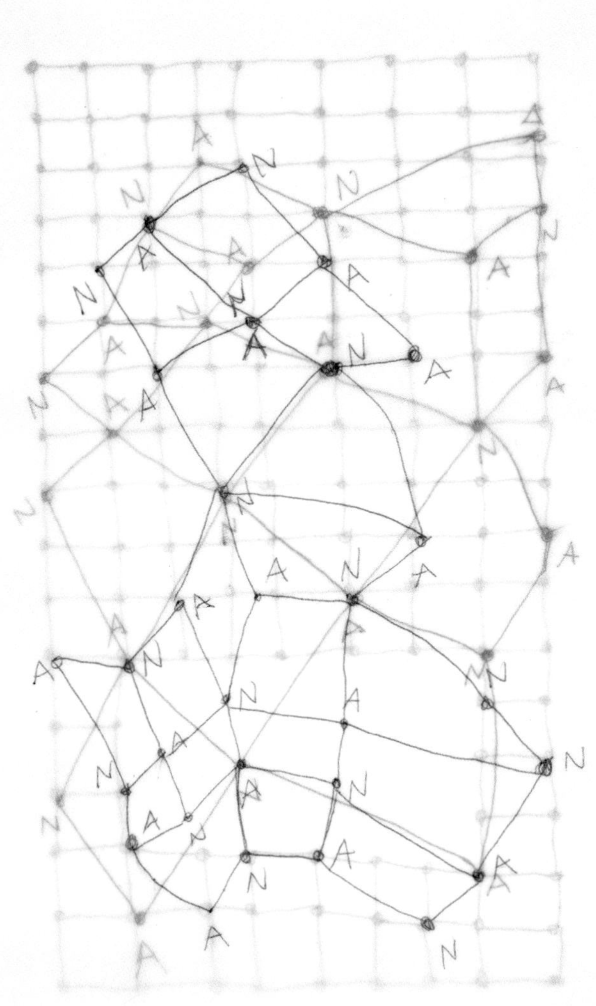

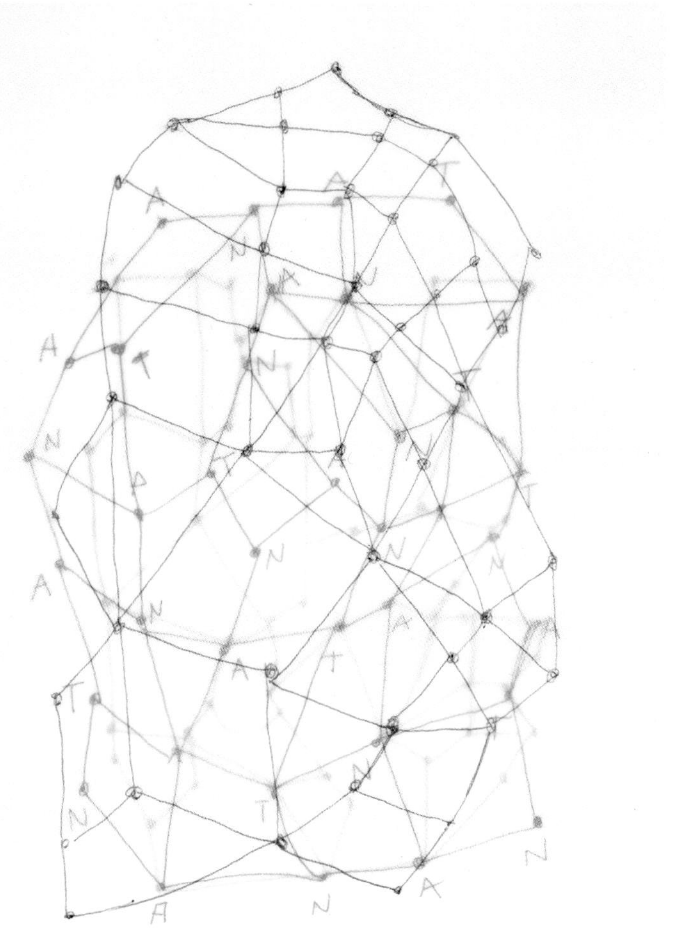

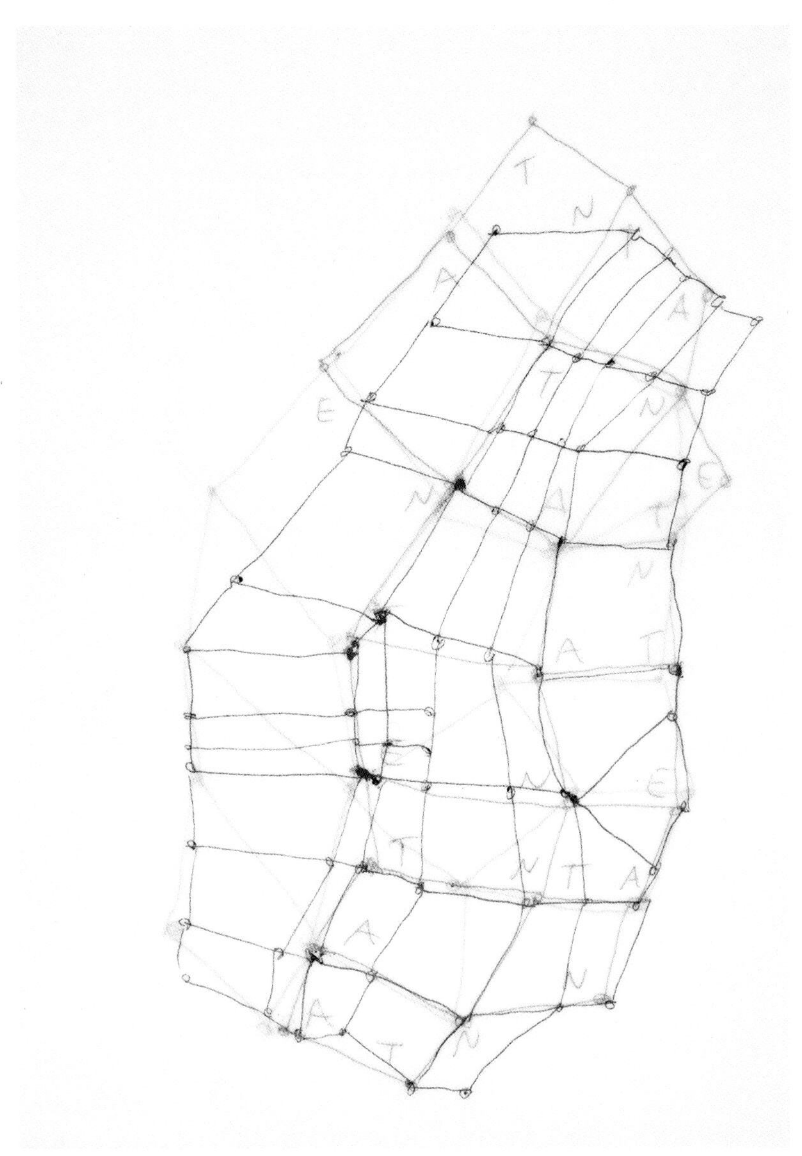

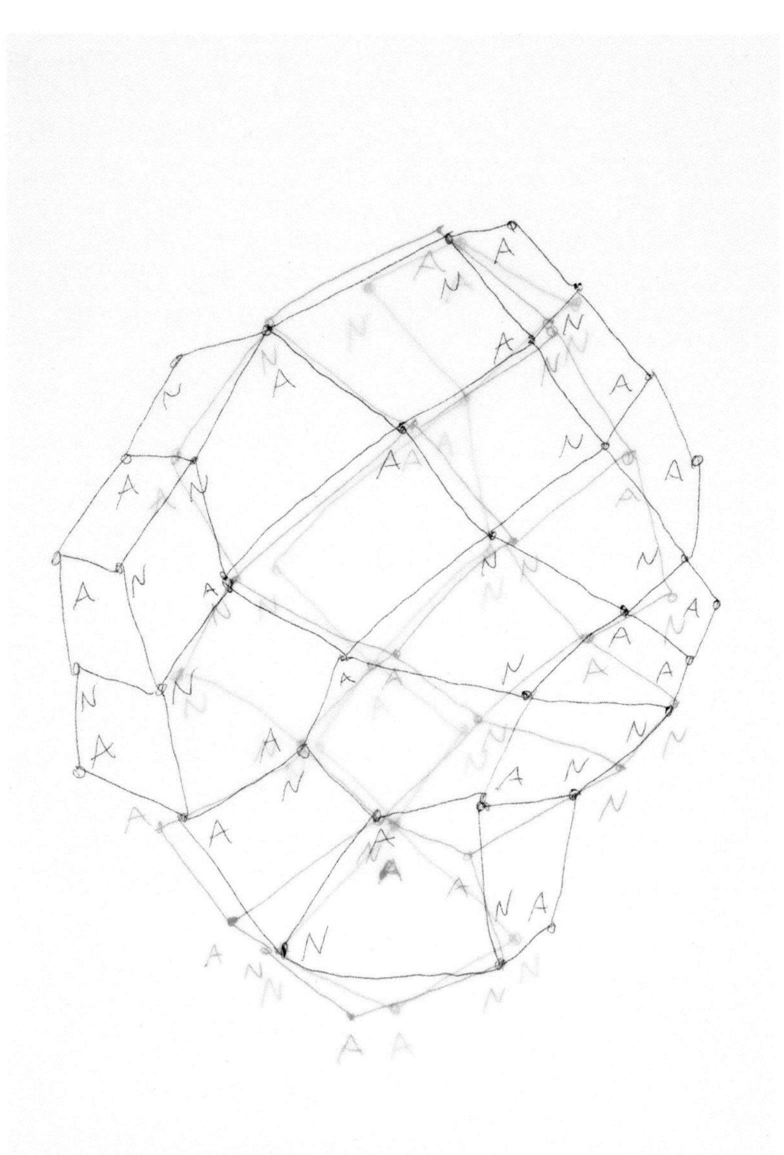

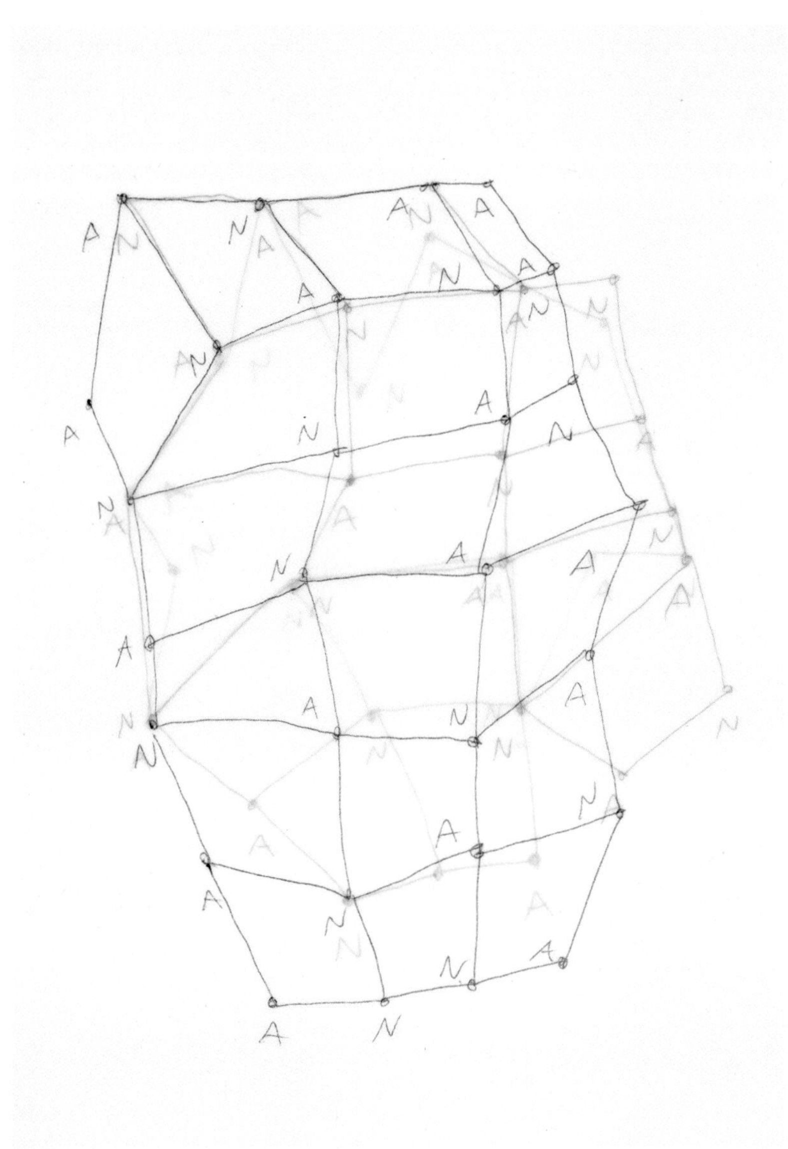

Stefan Weber

Grids of connections and breaking lights – Cairo and mashrabiyas in the museum

'I was always attracted to the abstract form of structures – that of molecules, DNA, or modules – those details in science that illuminate us about the bigger structure of life. I see similarities between my drawings, which are inspired by the shape of the mashrabiya and molecular structures, especially in the joins where the lines cross each other.'

Susan Hefuna has been working on the *Woman Cairo* series since 2003, with large format lattices in wood and other material (mashrabiyas) featuring gridwork inscriptions of the word 'woman'. They are produced by Cairene artisans with traditional production techniques. Works from this series can be found in various international art collections and museums and the Museum of Islamic Art in Berlin just acquired one example with the help of Alwaleed Philanthropies. This article will look into the history of mashrabiyas and its presentation in a collection of Islamic(ate) Art.

Mashrabiyas are a very specific element in architecture, iconic for Cairo and widespread in the Middle East. They are put together out of fine-turned wooden elements to appear as an almost kaleidoscopic grid. The rectangular screens are usually composed of alternating smaller regular sections of stars and geometric patterns. They are of different sizes for widows or room divisions – some several metres high and wide. Wooden grids are of course very common in history. They are by far not restricted to Egypt. A famous example from the early Islamic period is the outstanding minbar (pulpit for the Friday sermon) at the great mosque of Qairouan (Sidi Oqba) from the 9th century. Wonderfully carved and detailed, it follows late antique patterns in design and is completely different from the later works. From the 11th century on, one finds grid patterns made from small turned elements plugged together in furniture. These are stuck into intersecting joints that appear like small bulbs, which leads to a regular network and interplay of thinner and thicker levels of the all-over symmetrical geometrical design of lines and joints. Starting the 12th century, this form could be found in Syria, Turkey, and Iraq, and shortly thereafter in the Maghreb. The first surviving examples were commissioned by the famous ruler of Syria and Northern Iraq Nur ad-Din ibn Zengi (1118–1174), among them one for Friday Mosque in Hama from 1164 and one for Aleppo (563/1168–69), later brought by Salah al-Din to the Aqsa Mosque, where it was destroyed in 1969. Quite a few minbars are known from this period, probably connected to the new spread of Friday Mosques at the time (not one in each town, but one and later many in each quarter). The new fashion of a fine-drilled net of stars and squares became a transregional fashion, crossing geographical and political borders: the choir stalls of the 14th-century Split Cathedral at the Dalmatian Coast feature lattices similar to those of the Middle East. All these examples are elements of furniture from religious spaces. Less furniture from secular places has been preserved, but the same technique and design was likely widely used in non-religious spaces as well, as the throne of the Anatolian Rumseljuk Sultan Kaykhusraw III (1259–1263) indicates (today in the Ankara Ethnographic Museum).

Susan Hefuna is interpreting screens and not furniture. On historical pictures from Cairo, they dominate the street views. Many Ottoman houses (1517–1867) are marked by mashrabiyas on the outside and on the inner courtyard façades. The oldest known and preserved larger work of the above-described design goes back to Qairuan. However, the barrier for the space in front of the prayer niche (maqsura) was commissioned in the 11th century. Similar designs likely also existed in Cairo by then, but the oldest surviving large-scale mashrabiyas come a bit later: around the cenotaph in Sultan Qalawun's mausoleum (1285), in the Fatimid al-Salih Tala'i Mosque from the restoration after the earthquake of 1303, or the impressive division screen of the prayer hall of the Mosque of Amir Altinbugha al-Maridani (1340). These gridworks are not only nice to look at but also have a function: they serve as room dividers in mosques and mausoleums and for windows of houses or schools that face the street and courtyards. Here they control the movement of people and the incoming light, help regulate the indoor climate thanks to their airy shading and to the creation of small air vortices in the wind. They screen private life from the outside world without cutting the interior from the exterior: one may look out, but no one can see inside from the outside without getting close and being noticed. The atmosphere in rooms with large mashrabiyas is sparkling, sensitive, and warm – being inside a room furnished with mashariyas is a special touching experience as light and space interact and become fluid.

At the Museum of Islamic Art at the Pergamon Museum, we were – like many others – inspired by this experience. Several late Mamluk and early Ottoman examples are in our collection, and we decided to follow this inspiration in the 'Cairo – Centre on the Nile' hall for the new galleries (due in 2027). They will be used as room dividers to lay out an abstract alley of the old city of Cairo, controlling movement and playing with light and views. Throughout the new galleries, we present multiple offers of sensual, aesthetic and/or intellectual experiences for diverse audiences by age, personal preferences or social background. The multisensory experience of immersive spaces is very important to us. In the Cairo Hall, we play with the light of the mashrabiyas and Mamluk lamps. For kids and adults alike there will be a shadow theatre from Mamluk Cairo – the oldest in existence – where one can play shadow theatre and listen to stories from audio stations while sitting on a bench. At another spot in the socket of the showcase of our famous Mamluk glass bottle, small boxes will allow the public to discover painted glass sherds with motifs of horses and riders. These all will add to an overall atmosphere of discovery and temptation. The mashrabiyas will contextualise our premodern collection and strengthen a sensual and inspiring experience. Through our framing, we need to prevent essentialising or orientalising – our gallery is not Cairo, neither now nor then; it is a staged presentation in a museum – faithful to the objects, historical research, and experiences of people with connections to Cairo but transparent in its limitation to represent realities or a fixed cultural unit. To this end, we will break the reading of an eternal past using the diverse voices of today. Among others, we will feature contemporary efforts for cultural heritage and cultural preservation through interviews of Cairene women architects who are heroes of the old town renovation. They will address questions of provenance, cultural looting, and preservation, and will tell us their version of the old town and its problems. Susan Hefuna will add another contemporary female voice with her mashrabiya, accompanied by a picture and a quote. The inscription in the mashrabiya *Woman Cairo* is in agreement with the interviews of our colleagues from Cairo, widening the often male-dominated historiography of the Middle East. This addition of contemporary art in a museum of premodern culture follows a special approach that shall allow statements to connect the past to the present without blurring the difference between them. German-born Susan Hefuna is not part of the specific Cairene past but belongs to our global present with its many intertwined and hybrid realities. For all twenty-three of our galleries, we added a new category to our modular label system called 'Contemporary positions'. Susan Hefuna will provide the visitor with her viewpoint cited at the beginning of this article. Inspiring, unexpected and adding a new, very personal layer of experience.

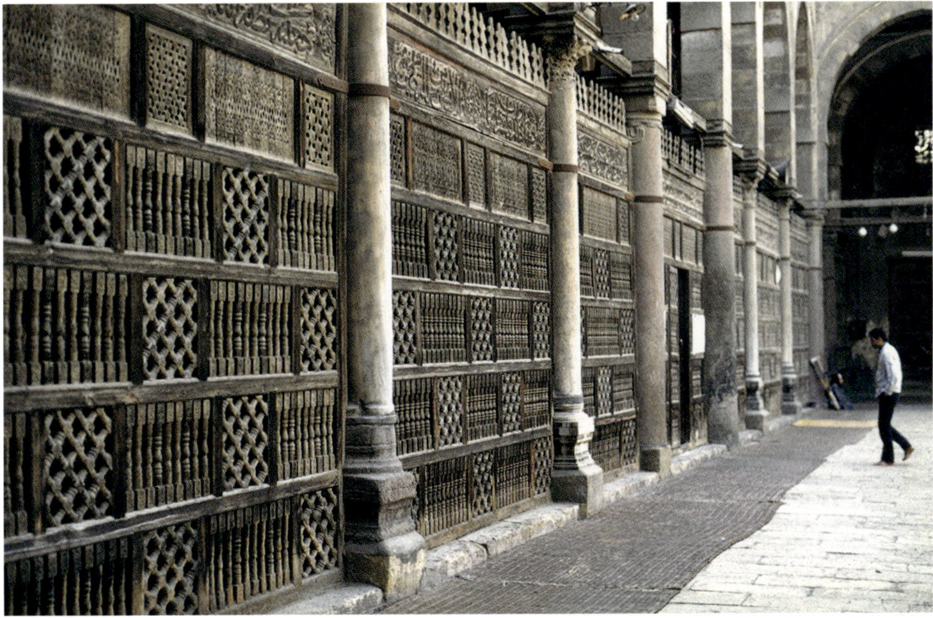

Cairo, mashrabiya in the courtyard of the Maridani Mosque, 1340

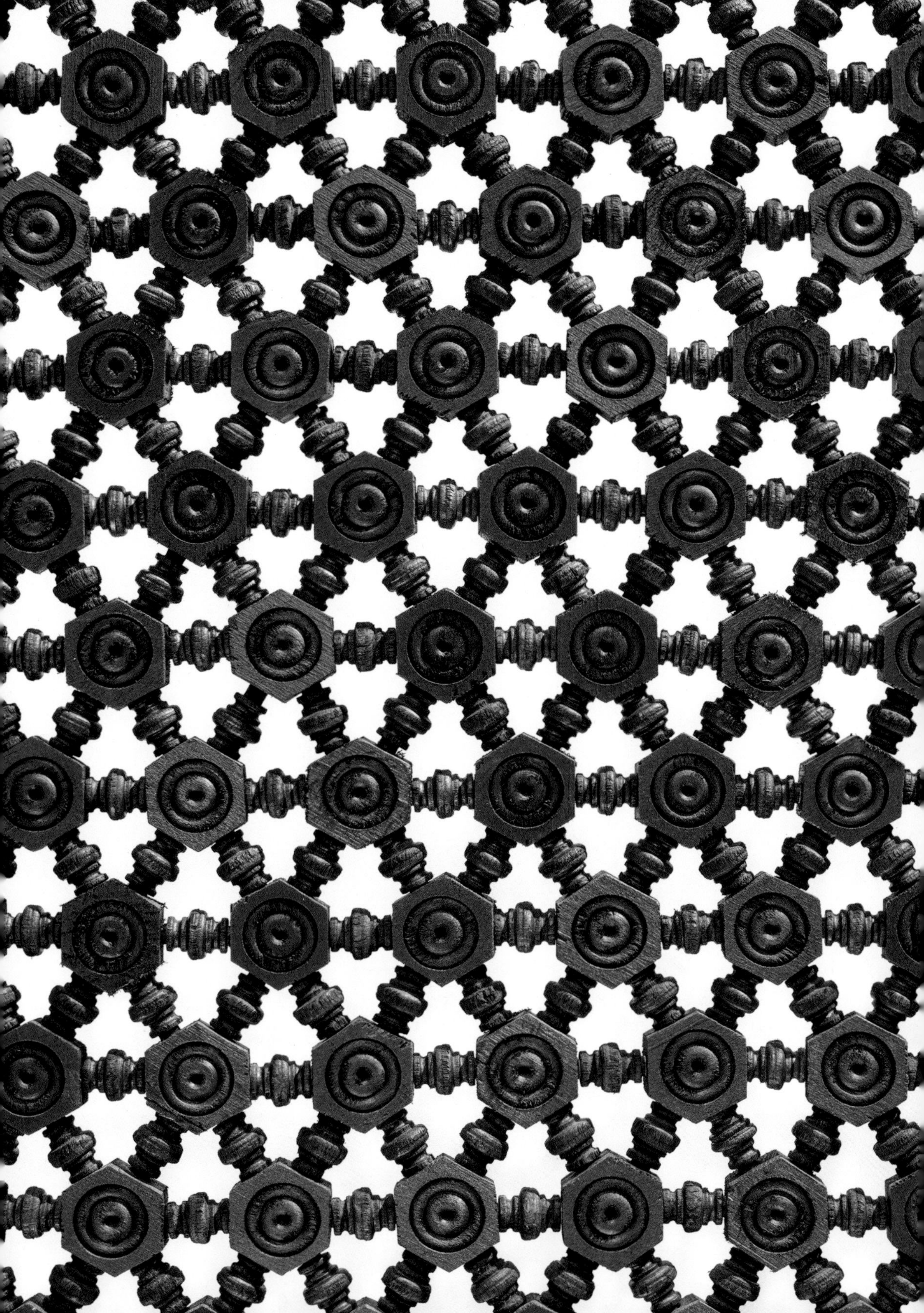

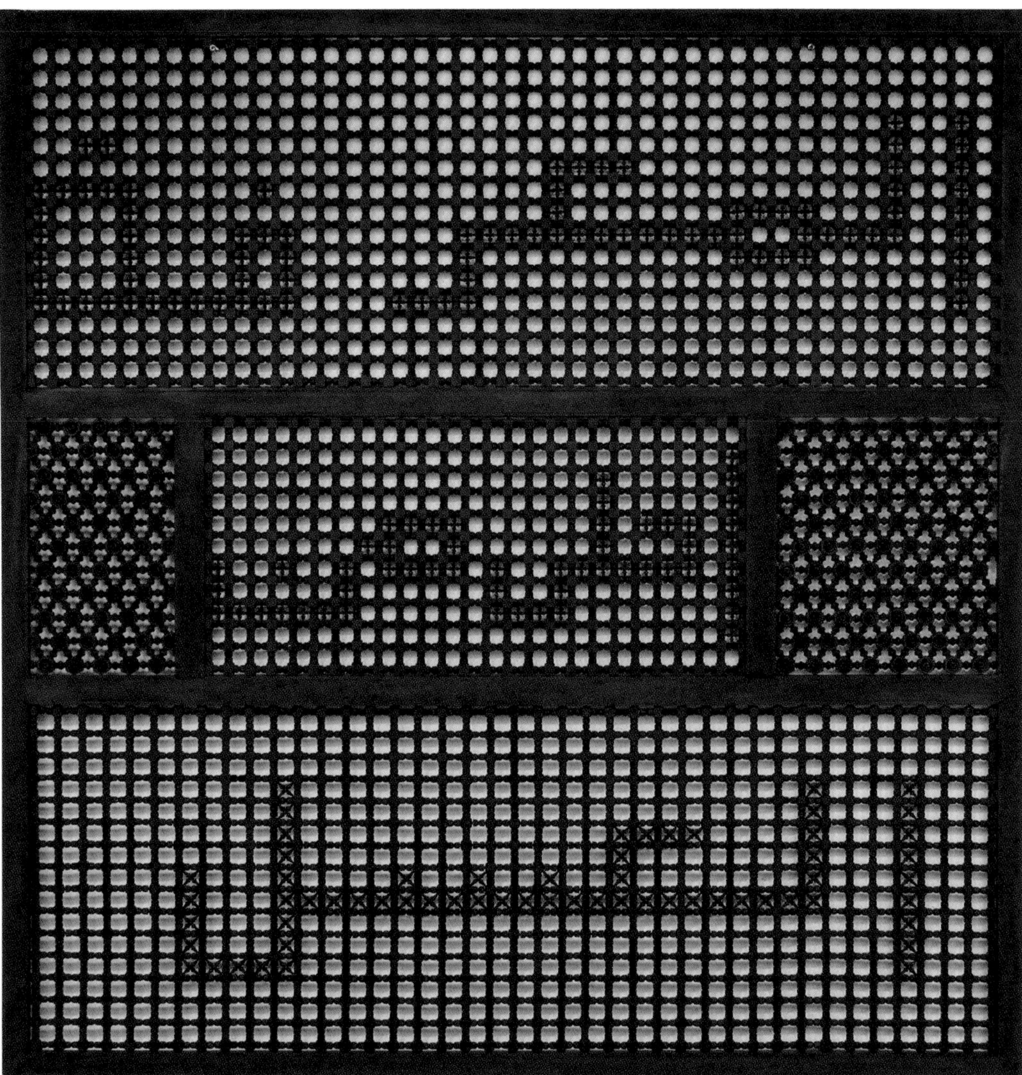

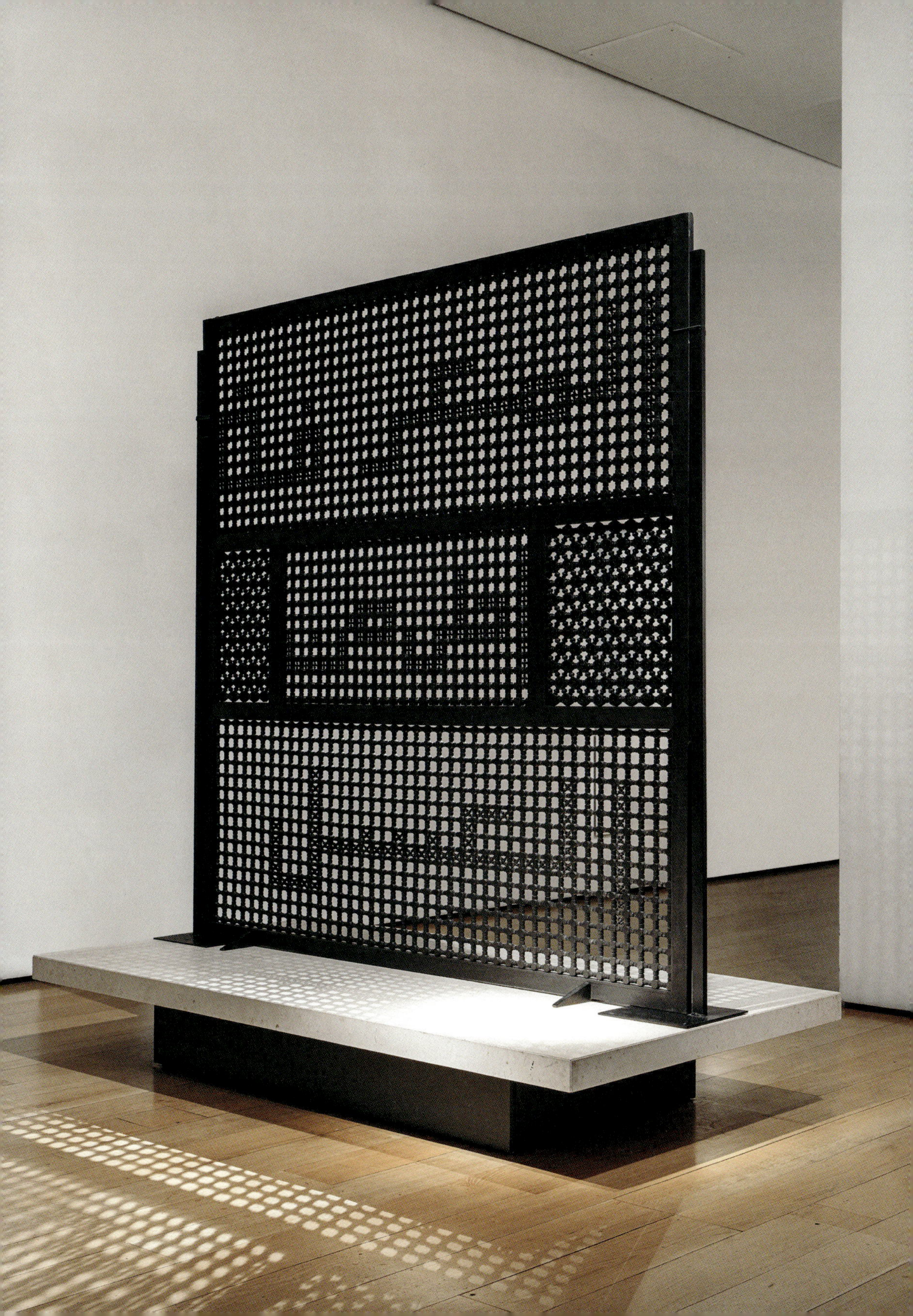

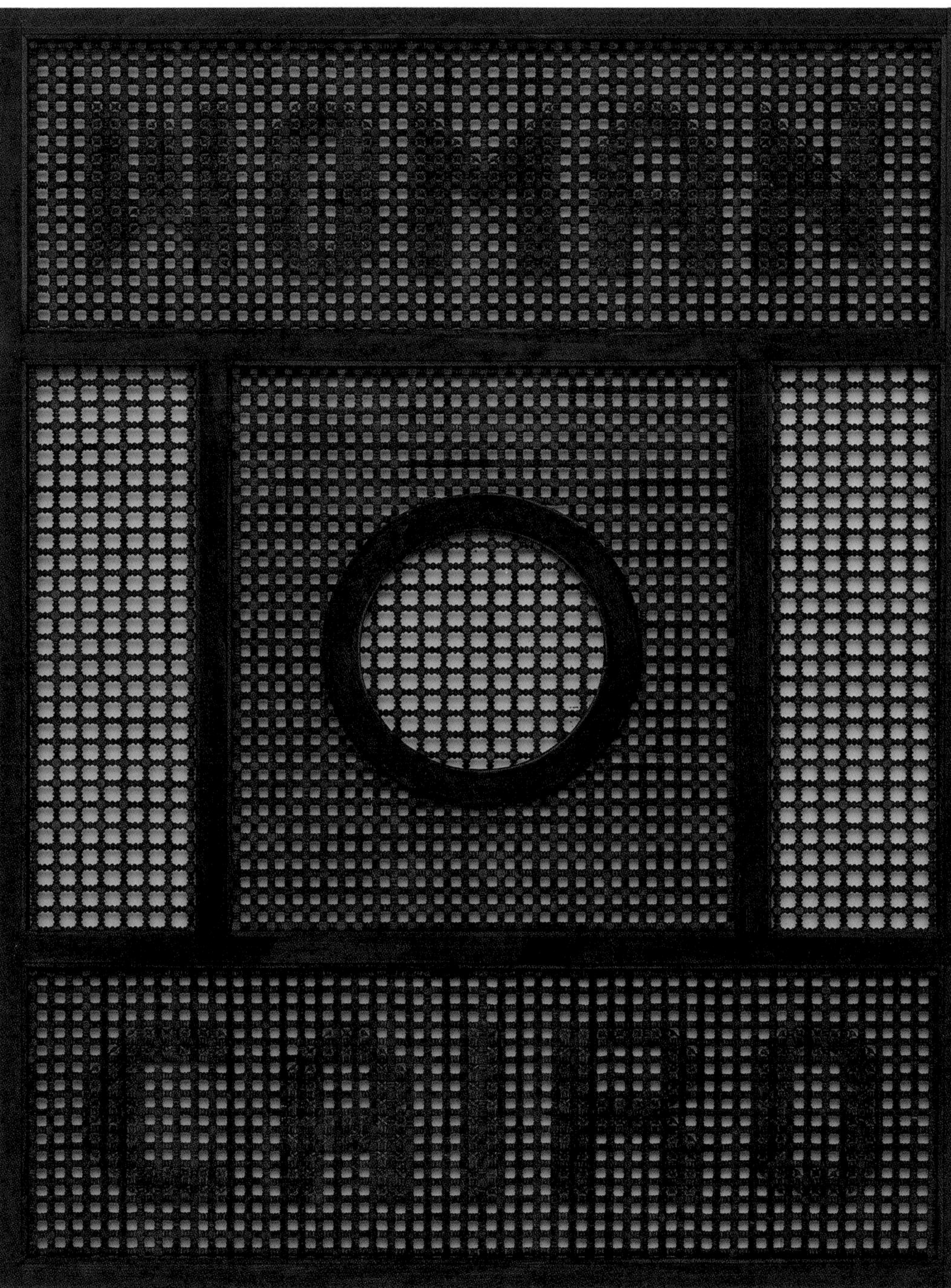

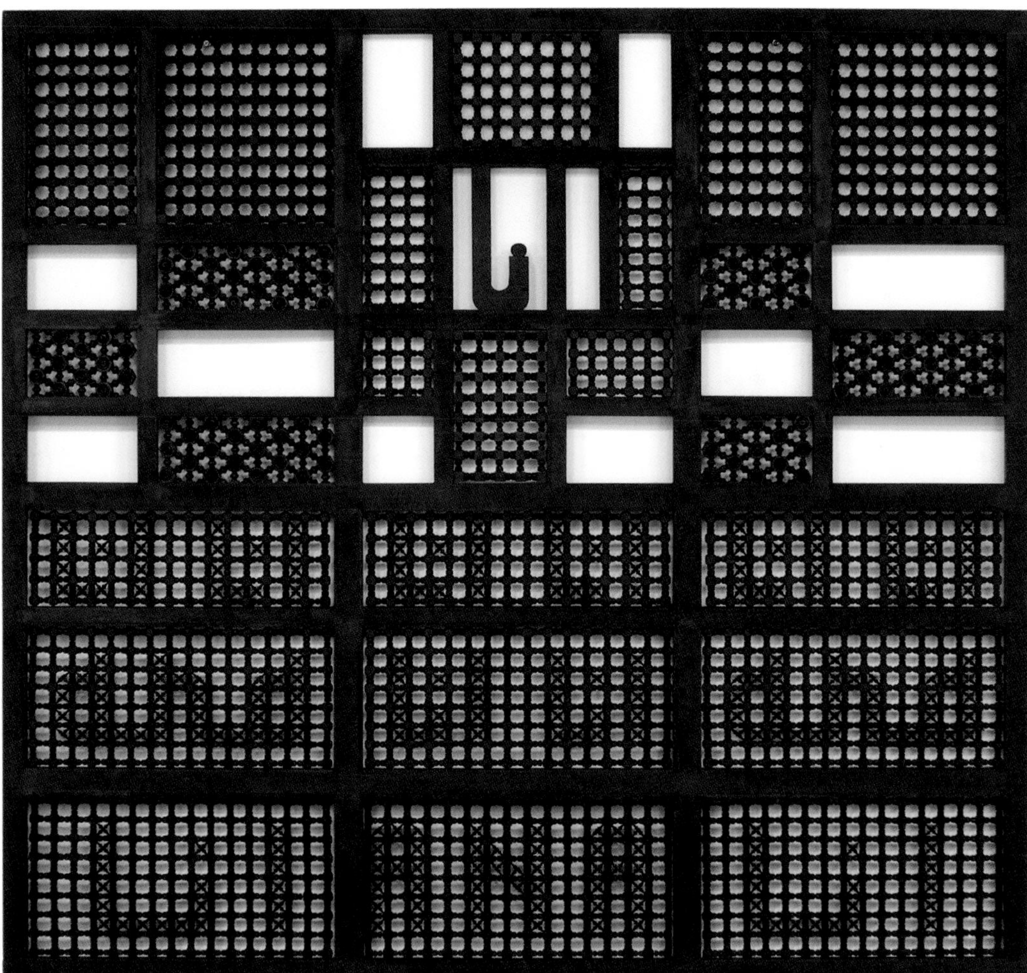

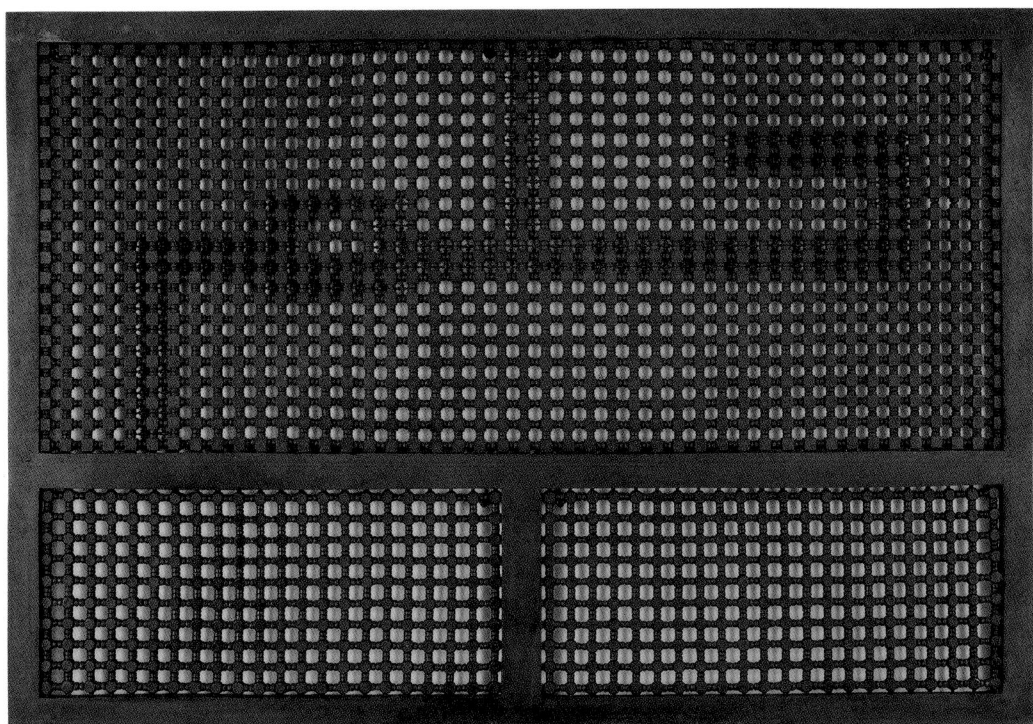

Index

Special thanks to:
The British Museum, London
Museum für Islamische Kunst in the Pergamonmuseum, Berlin

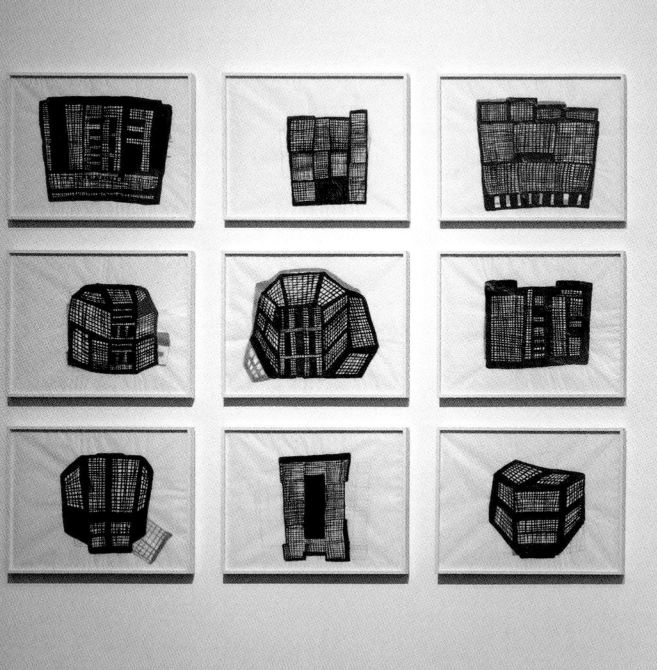
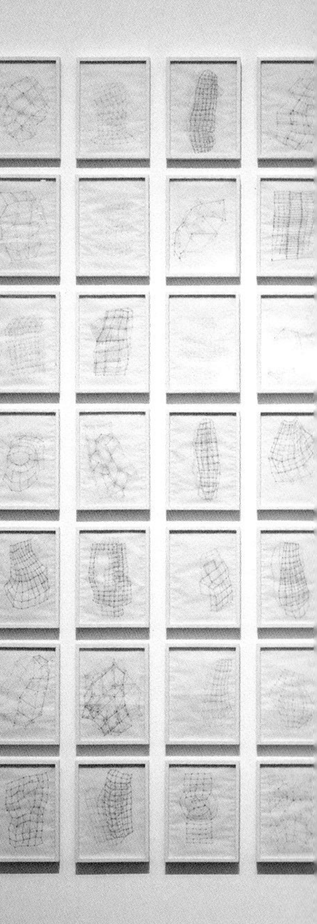

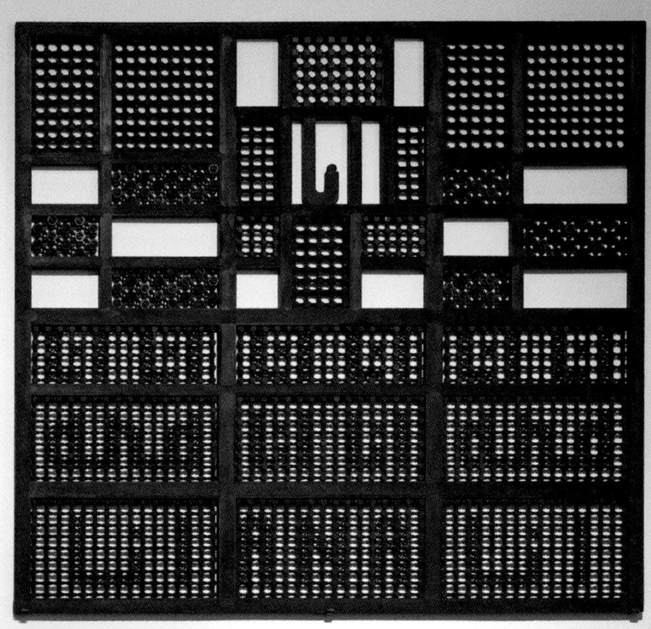

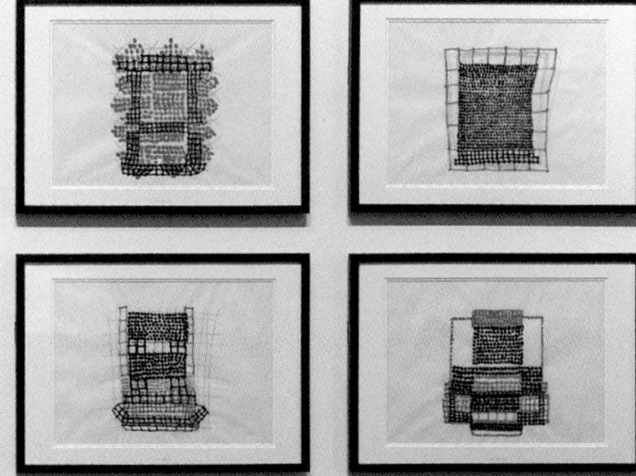

Project Management: Kehrer Verlag (Sylvia Ballhause)
Texts: Venetia Porter, Stefan Weber
Copy Editing: Elisabeth Buchet-Deák
Design: Kehrer Design (Laura Pecoroni)
Image Processing: Kehrer Design (René Henoch)
Production Management: Kehrer Design (Tom Streicher)

Photographs: Petra Jaschke (pp. 14–16, 33–57),
Achim Kukulies (pp. 21–29, 69, 73), Graham Waite (pp. 65, 71),
Francis Ware (pp. 3, 10, 13, 16, 18–19, 31, 63, 67, 78–79),
Stefan Weber © Friends of the Museum für Islamische Kunst
in the Pergamonmuseum e.V. (p. 61)

Bibliographic information published by the
Deutsche Nationalbibliothek
The Deutsche Nationalbibliothek lists this publication
in the Deutsche Nationalbibliografie; detailed bibliographic
data is available on the Internet at http://dnb.dnb.de.

Printed and bound in Germany
ISBN 978-3-96900-102-8

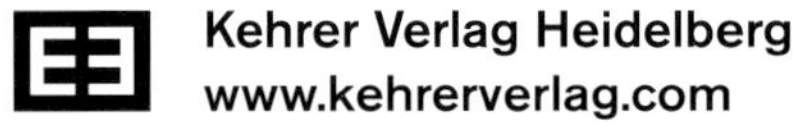

Kehrer Verlag Heidelberg
www.kehrerverlag.com